Angelo Cagnola

Analysis of the Gospels

Of the Sundays of the year

Angelo Cagnola

Analysis of the Gospels
Of the Sundays of the year

ISBN/EAN: 9783337282578

Printed in Europe, USA, Canada, Australia, Japan

Cover: Foto ©Thomas Meinert / pixelio.de

More available books at **www.hansebooks.com**

ANALYSIS OF THE GOSPELS

OF

THE SUNDAYS OF THE YEAR.

From the Italian of
ANGELO CAGNOLA.

BY
REV. L. A. LAMBERT, LL.D..
AUTHOR OF "NOTES ON INGERSOLL," "TACTICS OF INFIDELS," ETC.

NEW YORK, CINCINNATI, CHICAGO:
BENZIGER BROTHERS,
Printers to the Holy Apostolic See.
1892.

CONTENTS.

	PAGE
First Sunday of Advent,	7
Second Sunday of Advent,	11
Third Sunday of Advent,	16
Fourth Sunday of Advent,	21
Christmas Day,	24
Sunday within the Octave of Christmas,	30
New Year's Day.—The Feast of the Circumcision,	34
Feast of the Epiphany,	37
First Sunday after Epiphany,	42
Second Sunday after Epiphany,	45
Third Sunday after Epiphany,	49
Fourth Sunday after Epiphany,	54
Fifth Sunday after Epiphany,	57
Sixth Sunday after Epiphany,	61
Septuagesima Sunday,	64
Sexagesima Sunday,	69
Quinquagesima Sunday,	74
First Sunday of Lent,	78
Second Sunday of Lent,	83
Third Sunday of Lent,	88

CONTENTS.

	PAGE
Fourth Sunday of Lent,	93
Fifth Sunday of Lent, or Passion Sunday,	97
Palm Sunday,	104
Easter Sunday,	108
First Sunday after Easter,	115
Second Sunday after Easter,	119
Third Sunday after Easter,	124
Fourth Sunday after Easter,	128
Fifth Sunday after Easter,	133
Sunday within the Octave of the Ascension,	137
Pentecost Sunday,	140
First Sunday after Pentecost, or Trinity Sunday,	145
Second Sunday after Pentecost,	150
Third Sunday after Pentecost,	153
Fourth Sunday after Pentecost,	159
Fifth Sunday after Pentecost,	164
Sixth Sunday after Pentecost,	167
Seventh Sunday after Pentecost,	172
Eighth Sunday after Pentecost,	176
Ninth Sunday after Pentecost,	179
Tenth Sunday after Pentecost,	182
Eleventh Sunday after Pentecost,	185
Twelfth Sunday after Pentecost,	189
Thirteenth Sunday after Pentecost,	194
Fourteenth Sunday after Pentecost,	197
Fifteenth Sunday after Pentecost,	201
Sixteenth Sunday after Pentecost,	205

	PAGE
Seventeenth Sunday after Pentecost,	209
Eighteenth Sunday after Pentecost,	214
Nineteenth Sunday after Pentecost,	218
Twentieth Sunday after Pentecost,	223
Twenty-first Sunday after Pentecost,	227
Twenty-second Sunday after Pentecost,	230
Twenty-third Sunday after Pentecost,	233
Twenty-fourth and Last Sunday after Pentecost,	239

ANALYSIS OF THE GOSPELS OF THE SUNDAYS OF THE YEAR.

FIRST SUNDAY OF ADVENT.

Gospel: St. Luke xxi. 25-33.

AT that time, Jesus said to His disciples: "And there shall be signs in the sun, and in the moon, and in the stars, and upon the earth distress of nations, by reason of the confusion of the roaring of the sea and of the waves: men withering away for fear and expectation of what shall come upon the whole world. For the powers of heaven shall be moved and they shall see the Son of man coming in a cloud with great power and majesty. But when these things begin to come to pass, look up and lift up your heads: because your redemption is at hand. And He spoke to them a similitude: See the fig-tree and all the trees: when they now shoot forth their fruit you know that summer is nigh. So you also, when you shall see these things come to pass, know that the kingdom of God is at hand. Amen I say to you, this generation shall not pass away till all things be fulfilled. Heaven and earth shall pass away: but My words shall not pass away."

Question. What was the purpose of Our Lord in this discourse?

Answer. His purpose was to make known some of the events which are to precede the end of the world and to incite Christians to prepare for that general judgment which He will come to pass on the living and the dead, that is, on the just and the unjust.

Q. What are these signs which will be seen in the sun, moon, and stars?

A. Our Lord, in St. Matthew's Gospel, tells us that the sun shall be darkened, the moon shall no longer give her light, the stars shall fall from heaven, and the powers of heaven shall be moved.

Q. It will be thus in the natural order, but how can this be understood in the spiritual order?

A. In the darkening of the sun we can recognize the loss which the Church suffers by the persecutions of Anti-christ. In the obscuring of the moon we see the ruin produced in men by the decay of charity. Our Lord tells us that if these days be not shortened on account of the elect, none would be saved. The stars falling from heaven represent teachers and preachers of the law and the faith who have fallen away, like the stars dragged down by the dragon described in the Apocalypse. Lastly, in the dissolution of the forces of nature is represented the decay of the Christian virtues, and in the consternation of peoples is seen the disorder caused by the decay of good morals and the triumph of impiety.

Q. Why will the Son of God appear upon a cloud?

A. To manifest His glory and power; the clouds being in Scripture language a symbol of the divinity, the chariot, the throne of the omnipotence and majesty of God.

Q. In what other ways will the power and majesty of Jesus Christ be manifested?

A. His power will be shown forth in the resurrection of the dead, who will in a moment return to life at His command, on His appearance as Judge. He will be an object of joy to the just, of terror to the sinner, and of wonder to all; and lastly, His power and glory will appear in passing sentence, rewarding the good and punishing the impious—a sentence which none can escape.

Q. And how will His majesty be manifested?

A. It will shine forth in the resplendent light which will emanate from His body and be, perhaps, greater than on Thabor, when He appeared accompanied by angels and saints. His majesty will also appear in the splendor of His throne, in the luminous cross, in the sound of the trumpet, in the lightnings and thunders, in the earthquakes, and in all the portents which precede and foretell His coming.

Q. How are we to understand the words: "Look up and lift up your heads, because your redemption is at hand"?

A. By these words Our Lord invites His just to have courage and to hope, because these prodigies will make known to them that the time is at hand when they will be liberated from the miseries of life and the bonds of death to arise glorious and immortal, and enter soul and body into the happiness of heaven.

Q. Why should they know from these prodigies that the time of their liberation is at hand?

A. Because Our Lord promised that as the unfolding plants indicate the immediate coming of summer, so the prodigies foretold by Him indicate the immediate approach of the end of the world and the resurrection of the flesh; and the just, after so great tribulations, will receive the reward of their patience, their constancy, and their fidelity in the service of God.

Q. Of what does Our Lord speak when He says: "This generation shall not pass away till all things be fulfilled"?

A. According to the Gospel of St. Matthew, Our Lord, in the discourse of which the Gospel of to-day is but a part, spoke of two things, namely, the destruction of Jerusalem and the end of the world. Referring to the destruction of Jerusalem, Our Lord by "this generation" meant the Jews who lived in His own time. Referring to the end of the world, "this generation" means the whole human race. As His prediction regarding Jerusalem has been fulfilled by the overthrow of that city, so will His prediction regarding the end of the world be fulfilled. He has pledged His word and His word does not fail. The heavens and the earth shall pass away, but the word of Christ will not change.

Q. Why does the Church at the beginning of Advent direct our attention to this Gospel?

A. As in the Gospel of to-day we are reminded of that general judgment which Christ will pronounce on the last day, the Church directs our attention to the Gospel for three motives referable to that judgment.

Q. What is the first of these motives?

A. The first motive of the Church is to remind us how this same Jesus Christ, Whom in a short time we will admire in His humility lying in a manger for love of us, and to teach us the way to heaven, will one day descend on earth in awful majesty to demand account of the use we have made of His graces and gifts, and to judge us according to our actions.

Q. And what is the second motive?

A. The second motive of the Church is to incite us by a wholesome fear to prepare ourselves to receive Jesus Christ with love at His first coming, and forsake sin and obey His holy law, so that at His second coming we may appear with confidence, well prepared, at His tribunal.

Q. And what is the last motive?

A. It is to impress deeply on our minds the thought of the last judgment, for to avoid sin and excite ourselves to penance it is enough to know that one day all our actions will be judged. It is to make this thought of the last judgment useful and efficacious that the Church, with maternal solicitude, recalls it to our minds at the beginning and end of the ecclesiastical year, and frequently during the course of the year.

Q. What should we then do in this holy season of Advent?

A. We should meditate on the coming of Christ, *the Judge*, in order to prepare ourselves to commemorate the day when He came as *the Saviour*. We should often pray to the Child Jesus to be reborn and grow in our hearts with His holy grace. We should prepare in our hearts the way for Him by works of penance and piety, and above all by the use of the holy sacraments.

SECOND SUNDAY OF ADVENT.

Gospel: St. Matthew xi. 2–10.

AT that time, "When John had heard in prison the works of Christ, sending two of his disciples, he said to Him: Art thou He that art to come, or do we look for another? And Jesus making answer said to them: Go and relate to John what you have heard and seen. The blind see, the lame walk, the lepers are cleansed, the deaf hear, the dead rise again, the poor have the gospel preached to them: and blessed is he that shall not be scandalized in Me. And when they went their way, Jesus began to say to the multitudes concerning John: What went you out into the desert to see? a reed shaken with the wind? But what went you out to see? a man clothed in soft garments? Behold they that are clothed in soft garments are in the houses of kings. But what went you out to see? a prophet? Yea I tell you, and more than a prophet. For this is he of whom it is written: Behold I send My Angel before Thy face, who shall prepare Thy way before Thee."

Q. Where was St. John when he sent this embassy to Our Lord?

A. He was in prison, by order of the impious Herod, who was enraged by the reproofs the Baptist had given him on account of the incestuous life he was leading with Herodias, the wife of his brother Philip, Tetrarch of Trachonitis.

Q. Why did St. John send this embassy to Christ?

A. He sent it in order to give his disciples an opportunity of knowing Jesus Christ, and to convince them that He was truly the Messias foretold by the prophets and expected of nations.

Q. Had St. John any doubt of this?

A. It was his disciples who doubted; he himself was certain of the fact, because when baptizing Our Lord in the Jordan he had seen the Holy Ghost coming down upon Him in the form of a dove, and had heard the testimony of the Eternal Father, Who said from on high: "This is My beloved Son in Whom I am well pleased;" and He Himself had added: "Behold the Lamb of God, Who taketh away the sins of the world."

Q. Had the Jews reason to ask Jesus if He was the Messias?

A. They had reason both in regard to the times and to Christ Himself.

Q. Why in regard to the times?

A. According to the predictions of the prophets the expected Messias was to appear when the nations of the East had fallen under the power of one great empire, when the seventy weeks of years spoken of by Daniel, the prophet, were completed, and when the sceptre of absolute dominion had passed from the kingdom of Juda, as foretold by Jacob. Now, in the time of Christ all these predictions were fulfilled. The nations of the East had fallen under the power of the Roman empire, the seventy weeks of years were ended, and the sceptre had passed from the land of Juda, and the Israelites groaned under the yoke of the stranger. The Jews, therefore, had good reason in the time of Christ to expect the coming of the Messias.

Q. Had they reason to recognize Christ as the Messias?

A. In Him and in Him alone they should have recognized the Messias. In Him the most minute circumstances regarding the Messias were verified. And if the Hebrews, instead of expecting and desiring, through a misunderstanding, a warrior, a conqueror, an earthly and powerful prince, had given attention to what was foretold of His birth, growth, habits, actions, of His humiliations, sufferings, and death, they would have been compelled to recognize Him as the Messias.

Q. How did Jesus Christ prove that He was the promised Messias?

A. As actions prove the character of a man, Jesus Christ proved that He was the expected Messias by referring to His own actions as those described by the prophet Isaias in particular.

Q. Why do you say this?

A. Isaias had foretold that the expected Saviour would cure the lame, the blind, the leprous, the deaf and the mute, raise the dead and preach to the poor the way of salvation. Jesus Christ did all these things, and proved that He was the promised Messias by appealing to His own acts, which were precisely those described by the prophet. When the disciples of St. John asked Him: "Art thou He that is to come or look we for another?" He replied: "Go and relate to John what you have heard, and what you have seen with your own eyes."

Q. What did the disciples of St. John hear and see?

A. From the multitude that followed Jesus Christ they heard of the wonders worked by Him, and from Himself they heard the heavenly doctrine preached and eternal life announced; and as St. Luke tells us, they saw with their own eyes the miracles worked in their presence by the same Divine Redeemer Who, to convince them, was pleased to cure the blind, the lame, the deaf, the mute, and lastly raised the dead in their presence.

Q. What are we to say to all this?

A. That Christ did not fail to submit the most convincing proofs that He was the messenger of the Eternal Father, and that those who refused to recognize in Him the Saviour promised from the beginning of the world were blind, impious, and without excuse.

Q. Why did Christ say: "Blessed are those who shall not be scandalized in Me"?

A. His poverty, His lowliness, His sufferings, and death led carnal men to believe that He was anything but God. Therefore it was that He declared blessed those who would not permit themselves to be deceived by appearances, as did the doubting disciples of St. John, and who, notwithstanding His humiliation, should recognize Him as the true Messias and true God, annihilated for the salvation of the world. Blessed are we then who, taught not by flesh and blood, but by the grace of the Eternal Father, have recognized and adored the Crucified, the only Son of the living God.

Q. Why did Christ, Our Lord, praise St. John?

A. In order that those who heard Him, struck by the example of that great and wonderful man whom He called the angel sent by the Lord to prepare His way, might be still more confirmed in their faith.

Q. Why did He wait till St. John's disciples had gone before praising him?

A. That they might not relate to St. John the praises spoken by the Divine Master, lest they might think Him guilty of flattery; and to teach us that in praising the virtues of others we should be careful not to give occasion of pride to those we praise.

Q. What did Christ praise in St. John?

A. His strength of soul, that did not permit him to be puffed up by the applause of the multitude, nor to be discouraged by sufferings and persecution. He praised the austerity of his life, his detachment from the things of the world, and the greatness of the destiny of him who prepared the way for the Messias and announced the actual presence of the Saviour, Whom the ancient prophets had announced from afar.

Q. What should we learn from this day's Gospel?

A. We should learn from St. John to profit by every means compatible with our state or condition; to be always zealous followers and disciples of Jesus Christ; to cause His holy name to be praised, by laboring constantly in His service; not to be pliant as reeds to every wind of temptation; to flee from the luxuries of life and the pomps of the world, and lastly to show forth in our own lives the life of Jesus Christ, following His example and practising the virtues which He made the models of excellence.

THIRD SUNDAY OF ADVENT.

Gospel: St. John i. 19–28.

AT that time: "The Jews sent from Jerusalem priests and levites to John, to ask him: Who art thou? And he confessed, and did not deny; and he confessed: I am not the Christ. And they asked him: What then? Art thou Elias? And he said: I am not. Art thou the prophet? And he answered: No. They said therefore unto him: Who art thou, that we may give an answer to them that sent us? What sayest thou of thyself? He said: I am the voice of one crying in the wilderness: Make straight the way of the Lord, as said the prophet Isaias. And they that were sent were of the Pharisees. And they asked him, and said to him: Why then dost thou baptize, if thou be not Christ, nor Elias, nor the prophet? John answered them, saying: I baptize with water, but there hath stood One in the midst of you Whom you know not. The same is he that shall come after me, Who is preferred before me: the latchet of Whose shoe I am not worthy to loose. These things were done in Bethania beyond the Jordan, where John was baptizing."

Q. What was the object of the Pharisees in sending the priests and levites to St. John?

A. The Pharisees were learned in the law and the prophets, and they knew that the time of the promised Messias was near at hand. Knowing the angelic and wonderful life of St. John they very naturally concluded that he might be the promised Messias of God Whom they were expecting. They therefore sent priests and levites to St. John that they might have from himself reliable information on this important subject.

Q. Why did these messengers ask St. John if he were not Elias, after they had heard that he was not the Christ?

A. Elias did not die; he was taken up from the earth in a chariot of fire, and God said by the mouth of Malachy that He would send the prophet back to the world before the great and terrible day of the Lord. But the Jews did not understand rightly these words, and erroneously applied them to the coming of Christ as Redeemer when they should have applied them to His coming as the Judge of men. As they were expecting the Messias at that time, they, in view of the words of Malachy, looked for the return to the world of the prophet Elias. With this in their minds they very naturally asked St. John if he were Elias who was to prepare the way for the Saviour of Israel.

Q. And why did St. John say that he was not Elias when Christ declared he was?

A. "St. John," says Gregory the Great, "was filled with the spirit and virtue of Elias, but was not Elias in person. St. John, then, was right in denying that he was Elias in person, and Christ was right in calling him Elias in reference to the spirit and virtue for which he was conspicuous, and also because of his office of precursor. St. John was the Elias or precursor of Christ's first coming, as Elias is to be the precursor of Christ's last coming on earth."

Q. Why did St. John deny that he was even a prophet?

A. A prophet is one who foresees and foretells future events. In this sense St. John was not a prophet, because he did not foretell the coming of the Saviour, but announced His actual presence, and pointed Him out, when he said: "Behold the Lamb of God, Who taketh away the sins of the world." On this account he was greater than all the prophets, as Christ Himself declared in the Gospel of St. Matthew.

Q. Why did St. John, when urged to tell who he was, reply that he was the voice of one crying in the wilderness: "Make straight the way of the Lord"?

A. By his reply the Baptist informed them of the nature of his mission, and directed their attention to the prophecy of Isaias which foretold his coming, by quoting the words of the prophet: "Speak to the heart of Jerusalem, saith the Lord, and call aloud to her; be ye comforted, My people, for your evil is come to an end, *then shall be heard a voice of one crying in the wilderness, Prepare ye the way of the Lord, make straight His paths.*" He also gave them a striking proof of his great humility, for though he was promised by an angel, born by a prodigy of the Most High, and sanctified before his birth by the presence of the Redeemer, yet he merely says of himself: "I am the voice of one crying in the wilderness."

Q. Why did these messengers ask St. John why he baptized if he was not the Christ, nor Elias, nor the prophet?

A. These messengers were both learned and malignant. They knew from the Scriptures that the Messias was to baptize for the remission of sins, and that of no other man, saint or prophet, had such a prediction been made. They therefore wished impudently to reprove him as pretending to an authority and ministry which he was not authorized to assume.

Q. What reply did St. John make to this insult?

A. He answered with a gentleness in perfect keeping with the character of a minister of the Lord. He gave an account of his works, added what sufficed to enlighten them, and returned good for evil. He said that he baptized with water, that he came to show them the way to penance, to prepare them to receive the Saviour, that there was then in the midst of them One Who was to baptize in the Holy Ghost for the remission of sins, and that they did not know Him because they thought Him a poor, humble, common man.

Q. Is there nothing else to be observed in the reply of St. John?

A. We must note the testimony given by him in favor of Jesus Christ. St. John said of Him in effect: "He is the Person Who will come after me, Who will wash away your sins and sanctify you. He is greater than I, and before me, and I am not worthy to loosen the latchets of His shoes." In this way he pointed out the Saviour, and left them without any pretext in not recognizing Jesus Christ as the Messias.

Q. Where did this event take place?

A. On the eastern bank of the Jordan opposite to Galgal, in a place called Bethany or Bethabara, the place where the Hebrews pitched their tents by command of Josue, before they passed over to enter the Promised Land. St. John, who preached penance and passing from a state of sin to a state of grace, chose this place from whence the chosen people passed from their wanderings in the desert to the abundance of the Land of Promise.

Q. What are we to learn from St. John?

A. We should learn to practise humility as he did, by confessing sincerely our nothingness, by not sounding our own praises even when there may be occasion to do so without danger of ostentation, and by suffering with patience injurious words even when performing faithfully our duties.

Q. Is there any other lesson for us in the example of St. John?

A. Yes, we should consider what our own answer will be when, like St. John, we are asked: "Who art thou?" Grant, O Lord, that we may be able to answer when the time comes: "We are Christians." Lastly, let us apply to ourselves these words: "Make straight the way of the Lord." Let us make every effort to prepare for the spiritual new-birth of Jesus Christ in our souls.

FOURTH SUNDAY OF ADVENT.

Gospel: St. Luke iii. 1-6.

AT that time: "In the fifteenth year of the reign of Tiberius Cæsar, Pontius Pilate being governor of Judea, and Herod being tetrarch of Galilee, and Philip, his brother, being tetrarch of Iturea and the country of Trachonitis, and Lysanias tetrarch of Abilina, under the high-priests Annas and Caiphas: the word of the Lord was made unto John, the son of Zachary, in the desert. And he came into all the country about the Jordan, preaching the baptism of penance for the remission of sins, as it is written in the book of the words of Isaias the prophet: A voice of one crying in the wilderness: Prepare ye the way of the Lord: make straight His paths. Every valley shall be filled: and every mountain and hill shall be brought low: and the crooked shall be made straight, and the rough ways plain. And all flesh shall see the salvation of God."

Q. Why did the Evangelist give so minute a description of the rulers and high-priests living at the time when St. John preached?

A. He did so for three reasons: First, to clearly establish the time and year in which the promised precursor of the Messias was to appear and with him Jesus Christ Himself.

Q. What was the second reason?

A. To show that the Redeemer had manifested Himself to the world at the precise time prophesied by the patriarch Jacob sixteen hundred and thirty years before. The time foretold was when the sceptre should pass from Israel into the hands of strangers, as were Tiberius Cæsar, Lysanias, and the two brothers

Herod Antipas and Philip, sons of the Idumian Herod who commanded the slaughter of the Innocents.

Q. What was the third reason?

A. The third reason why St. Luke wrote so minutely of the rulers and high priests was to show the part taken by them in the history of Christ. Tiberius ruled the Roman Empire at the time of Christ's preaching and death. It was he who, struck by Christ's miracles and sanctity, sought to have His name enrolled among the gods of the empire. Pilate, his procurator in Judea, pronounced the sentence of death after he had so solemnly declared Christ's innocence. Herod, who could not find Him guilty, considered Him a madman, and Philip put John the Baptist to death. Lastly, Annas and Caiphas, the high-priests, were the leaders of the enemies of Christ, Whom they persecuted even to the cross.

Q. What is the meaning of the words: "The Lord spoke to John in the desert"?

A. God had prepared John for the great office of precursor of His Christ. Promised by the message of an angel, born of a mother sterile and advanced in years, sanctified before his birth, glorified by prodigies at his birth, enriched with heavenly virtues, John lived amid the horrors of the desert a model of penance, an angel rather than a man. In the fulness of time God invested him with his mission and urged him to raise his voice, preach penance, and announce the presence of the Saviour.

Q. In what desert did St. John preach?

A. In that desert which lies between the east bank of the Jordan and the desert of Arabia, the same through which the Hebrews passed when, after the captivity of Babylon, they returned to their country to set about rebuilding the temple.

Q. Why is it said: "It is written in the book of the words of Isaias"?

A. Because when Isaias praised that glorious passage of the Hebrews his words had a twofold meaning; while he praised the liberation of the people from the captivity of Babylon he also predicted the liberation of the human race from the chains of sin and from the slavery of Satan—a liberation that was one day to be proclaimed in this same desert.

Q. What were the words of Isaias?

A. They were these: "The voice of one crying in the desert: Prepare ye the way of the Lord, make straight in the wilderness the paths of our God. Every valley shall be exalted and every mountain and hill shall be made low, and the crooked shall become straight and the rough ways plain, and all flesh shall see the salvation of God."—*Isaias* xl. 3.

Q. To whom did Isaias refer?

A. By the words: "The voice of one crying in the desert," he referred to John the Baptist, who made his voice heard in the desert solitude between the Jordan and Chaldea. He cried: "Prepare ye the way of the Lord," that is, correct your ways, do penance.

Q. And how are the other words to be explained?

A. Isaias, in foretelling that the valleys would be filled up, the mountains made low, and the crooked ways straight, announced that the grace of God would remove all obstacles that make our salvation difficult: that by means of grace the weak and lowly would be filled with heavenly strength; that the proud would be humbled; that the erring would return to the straight path; that our affections would be regulated and our passions overcome. The history and annals of the Church show that this prophecy has been fulfilled.

Q. Why is it said that "all men shall see the salvation of God"?

A. Because by the apostles and their successors the gospel would be spread throughout the world, as in fact it is.

Q. What are we to learn from all this?

A. First, we should be strengthened in our holy faith by considering that everything regarding it had been prepared, foretold, and completed by the wisdom, power, and goodness of God. We should also learn from the words of St. John that the only means of participating in the graces of the nativity of Our Lord is to do sincere penance for sins committed, reform our ways, and return to God with all the affections of our heart.

CHRISTMAS DAY.

Gospel: St. Luke ii. 1–14.

"AND it came to pass that in those days there went out a decree from Cæsar Augustus, that the whole world should be enrolled. This enrolling was first made by Cyrinus, the governor of Syria. And all went to be enrolled, every one into his own city. And Joseph also went up from Galilee out of the city of Nazareth into Judea, to the city of David, which is called Bethlehem, because he was of the house and family of David, to be enrolled with Mary, his espoused wife, who was with child. And it came to pass that when they were there, her days were accomplished that she should be delivered. And she brought forth her first-born Son, and wrapped Him up in swaddling-clothes, and laid Him in a manger, because there was no room for them in the inn. And there were in the same country shepherds watching, and keeping the night-watches over their flock. And behold, an angel of the Lord stood by them, and the brightness of God shone round about them, and they feared with a great fear. And the angel said to them: Fear not; for behold I bring you good tidings of great joy, that shall be to all the people. For this day is born to you a Saviour, Who is Christ the Lord, in the city of David. And this shall be a sign unto you: You shall find the Infant wrapped in swaddling-clothes, and laid in a manger. And suddenly there was with the angel a multitude of the heavenly army, praising God, and saying: Glory to God in the highest, and on earth peace to men of good will."

Q. What emperor ordered the census and description of the subjects of the empire to be taken?

A. Cæsar Octavianus Augustus, a grand-nephew of Julius Cæsar. Having overcome his rival, Antony, at the battle of Actium, Augustus became the sole master of the Roman Empire, and ruled long in peace, glory, and unexampled prosperity.

Q. Why did Augustus order a census to be taken?

A. Finding himself at peace on all sides and his treasury exhausted by the preceding wars, he wished not only to satisfy his curiosity and ambition by knowing the number of his subjects, but also to replenish his treasury by the tribute which each one had to pay on that occasion. Whatever may have been the purpose of Augustus, his command was a wise disposition of God, that the Jews as well as the Gentiles might easily and with certainty know that the Messias, according to the predictions of the prophets, had been born in Bethlehem of the house and family of David, the son of Jesse the Bethlemite.

Q. How did this enrolment enable the Jews and Gentiles to know of the birth of the Messias?

A. It must be remembered that about this time a rumor prevailed in Syria and Judea that a king was about to be born who was to become the ruler of the world. This rumor from Asia came to Rome and so alarmed the senate that it decreed that nourishment should be denied to all male children born during the consulate of Antony and Cicero. This decree, however, had no effect, on account of the opposition to so barbarous a law. Besides this rumor, the oracles of the sibyls had led even the Gentiles to expect a great king, the son of an immortal king, holy and victorious. The Gentiles being influenced by these rumors and predictions, and the empire being at peace, attention was more easily directed to the slaughter of the children ordered by Herod for the purpose of destroying the new-born King of the Jews. Thus it happened that the name of Jesus, on the day of His circumcision, was inscribed on the records of the census which, as Tertullian informs us, were sent to Rome and preserved in the public archives there. This would necessarily make known to the world the birth of Jesus Christ and the appearance of the expected Messias. It was then proper, says the venerable Bede, that the King of peace who came to reconcile man with God should be born at a time when peace reigned throughout the world.

Q. You say: "According to the predictions of the prophets." Did any prophet foretell this universal peace at the birth of the Redeemer?

A. The peace which prevailed at the birth of the promised Messias had been predicted by the prophet Isaias in these words: "And they shall turn their swords into plough-shares and their lances into pruning hooks; people will not rise against people, the unarmed arm, nor will they wage war." The profound peace that prevailed in the days of Augustus is known to all. It was called "the Octavian peace."

Q. Why did Joseph, who dwelt in Nazareth, have to go to Bethlehem to be enrolled?

A. The Hebrew nation was divided into tribes and the tribes were divided into families. The decree of the emperor required the census to be taken according to tribes and families. Hence each one had to inscribe his name at the city or place of his origin, where his ancestors or the head of the family had lived. Joseph was of the tribe of Juda and of the house of David. David, the son of Jesse, was born in Bethlehem, and Joseph, as a descendant of the royal house of David, had to go to that town to have his name inscribed. This was also an admirable disposition of Divine Providence, that the whole world might know that Jesus Christ was born in Bethlehem, that he descended from the house or family of David and from the tribe of Juda, as foretold by the prophets, and that, therefore, he should be acknowledged as the true and expected Messias.

Q. Had Joseph to make a long journey?

A. He had to make a journey of over seventy miles. Leaving the tribe of Zabulon he passed through the tribes of Issachar, Manasses, between the Red Sea and the Jordan, Ephrem and Benjamin, till he came to the tribe of Juda, in which is Bethlehem, six miles from Jerusalem. We learn from St. Joseph submission and obedience to the laws of those who govern us, and whose authority comes from God.

Q. If Mary was about to give birth to her divine Son, why did she accompany St. Joseph on so long a journey?

A. The prophet, Micheas, had foretold that the Messias would be born in Bethlehem of Juda, and the word of God pronounced by the lips of that inspired man must be fully verified. The word "Bethlehem" signifies "the House of Bread," and it was proper that from that house should come He Who is the heavenly bread, He Who nourishes our souls with His doctrines, His grace, and His flesh.

Q. Why did the holy Mother place the Child in a manger?

A. Perhaps on account of the poverty of Joseph, or perhaps because of the great number of people in the small town of Bethlehem, the holy Virgin could not find lodgings, and was compelled to take refuge in a stable, and having no better place, laid the Infant in the manger from which the cattle fed.

Q. Does the Evangelist say that there were an ox and an ass at this manger?

A. On this as on some other things he is silent. This belief is, however, so common that the Church applies in this sense the words of the prophet Habacuc: "You will be known in the midst of animals," and explains in this sense the words of Isaias: "The ox will know his owner, and the ass will know the manger of his Lord." St. Gregory of Nyssa says the ox was a figure of the Hebrew people, accustomed to carry the yoke of the law, and that the ass was a figure of the Gentiles carrying the burden of their superstitions and sins. As the ox and the ass rested in the stall without yoke or burden and partook of food, so in like manner the Hebrews as well as the Gentiles were called to rest in the presence of Christ; the former to throw off the yoke of the Old Law, the latter to free themselves from the burden of error and sin, and both to partake, in Him, of the food of eternal life.

Q. Why were the shepherds called first to the manger?

A. The shepherds followed the custom of the ancient patriarchs and watched while others slept; they were poor and earned their bread by their labor; they lived like the primitive Christians who watched over themselves while others slept idly in the pleasures of the world. Those who are poor in spirit and suffer with patience the inconveniences of poverty will be preferred by Our Lord, and be called by Him to the happiness of heaven.

Q. What lesson should we learn from Jesus in the manger?

A. A thousand things, but principally contempt for riches and the pomps and honors of the world. Jesus, the Master of the universe, born poor and in a stable; Jesus, the most innocent of beings, to suffer at His very birth; Jesus, the adored of angels, humiliating Himself in a manger as the least of the living. With such an example before us, who would prefer the riches, the pleasures, and the pomps of this transitory world to the eternal joys promised by the Son of God?

SUNDAY WITHIN THE OCTAVE OF CHRISTMAS.

Gospel: St. Luke ii. 33-40.

"AND His father and mother were wondering at those things which were spoken concerning Him. And Simeon blessed them, and said to Mary His mother: Behold this Child is set for the fall and for the resurrection of many in Israel, and for a sign which shall be contradicted. And thy own soul a sword shall pierce, that out of many hearts thoughts may be revealed. And there was one Anna, a prophetess, the daughter of Phanuel, of the tribe of Aser: she was far advanced in years, and had lived with her husband seven years from her virginity. And she was a widow until four score and four years: who departed not from the temple, by fasting and prayers serving night and day. Now she at the same hour coming in, confessed to the Lord; and spoke of Him to all that looked for the redemption of Israel. And after they had performed all things according to the law of the Lord, they returned into Galilee, to their city of Nazareth. And the Child grew, and waxed strong, full of wisdom: and the grace of God was in Him."

Q. What are we told in particular in to-day's Gospel?

A. We are told of the predictions of Simeon and Anna, made when the Child Jesus was presented in the temple in compliance with the law which required this presentation of every first-born.

Q. Why does this Gospel, when speaking of Joseph, call him father, and why did Joseph and Mary wonder at the things they heard?

A. It is a truth of faith that Jesus Christ as man had no father. He was born of Mary ever a virgin, as well during as after His birth; but as Joseph was reputed by all who were ignorant of the great mystery to be the natural father of Jesus Christ, and as, says St. Augustine, he had over Him the authority of a father, the Gospel in this place calls him father. St. Joseph and Mary wondered at the things they heard from Simeon and Anna, for it was indeed surprising to hear those persons instructed by the Holy Ghost about those things which regarded the Divinity, describing the character and future life of Jesus Christ.

Q. Whom did Simeon bless, and what was his blessing?

A. Simeon recognized in Jesus Christ the Son of the Eternal Father, and therefore adored and glorified Him and awaited His blessing and the application of His merits and grace. He then did not bless Christ; he blessed Joseph and Mary, to whom he foretold the heavenly favors and graces relative to their high office and to the arduous duties imposed on them.

Q. How could Simeon say that Jesus Christ would be the occasion of the fall and resurrection of many in Israel?

A. These words of Simeon correspond with the words in which Isaias predicted that the future Messias would be the cause of the sanctification of some and for others a stumbling-block and an occasion of scandal. The fact then makes the prediction evident, since it is seen that many, believing in Christ, will rise from the death of sin and obtain eternal life, and others will be obstinate in their blindness, fall into greater sins, and cast themselves by their obstinacy of heart into the abyss of perdition.

Q. What did Simeon mean when he said Christ was set " for a sign that shall be contradicted "?

A. According to the best interpreters, among whom are Origen, St. Basil, and Tertullian, the word *sign* means the same as prodigy or portent. In this sense the generation, life, doctrines, miracles, passion, death, and resurrection of Jesus Christ are a prodigy and a portent which could never have been imagined by the human mind. This prodigy many have believed, and many have contradicted it so far as to crucify Him and continue to persecute Him, ever sitting at the right hand of the Father in heaven. It is in this light we should consider the words of Simeon; in this light His prophecy has been verified.

Q. What is this sword that was to pierce the soul of Mary?

A. The sword of grief and sorrow, by which at the foot of the cross she became the Queen of martyrs. Let us admire here the strength of soul and resignation to the will of heaven shown by Mary, who was not disturbed by so sad a prophecy. Let us learn from her to accept with silent resignation the tribulations which it may please God to permit us to see approaching.

Q. Who was the woman who "departed not from the temple"?

A. An aged woman called Anna, the daughter of Phanuel, a man of renown even after his death. She was married when young; after seven years her husband died, and she remained a widow, leading a devout life to the age of eighty-four years, in the highest public esteem.

Q. What did she do in the temple?

A. It is believed that she dwelt in apartments adjoining the temple and instructed and directed in virtue the young maidens sent there by their pious parents, directing them by her good example, her piety, and her prayers. Blessed are those who imitate her example in directing souls to God!

Q. What did Anna say of Christ, and to whom did she speak?

A. She said that the Child was indeed the expected Messias, the Son of God, clothed in our flesh; that He came to take away the sins of the world and to redeem the human race from the slavery of Satan and from eternal death. All this she told to those pious souls who, resting on the faith of the patriarchs and trusting in the promises of the prophets, believed and hoped in the Christ to come, and awaited from Him the redemption of afflicted Israel.

Q. What should we learn from this account for our spiritual benefit?

A. These old people, Simeon and Anna, led a holy life, and always believed in and hoped for Jesus Christ to come. They obtained the grace to see Him with their own eyes and to press Him to their breasts, and at the proper time were enlightened by the Holy Ghost to recognize Him and announce Him to others.

Q. And what do you conclude from all this?

A. That if we begin from childhood to lead a holy life and persevere, as they did, in good works, we can, like them, press to our breasts Jesus Christ in spirit and truth; we will obtain light, and be able to make Him known to many. And lastly, at the end of our lives we shall be contented and resigned, as Anna and Simeon were, and be able to say with them that we die happy, because death for us is the passage to eternal beatitude.

NEW YEAR'S DAY.—THE FEAST OF THE CIRCUMCISION.

Gospel: St. Luke ii. 21.

"AND after eight days were accomplished that the Child should be circumcised, His name was called Jesus, which was called by the angel, before He was conceived in the womb."

Q. What do the few words of the Gospel of to-day refer to?

A. We are told that on the eighth day after His birth the Infant Jesus, in fulfilment of the law was circumcised, and that He was called Jesus, as had been foretold by the Archangel Gabriel when he announced to Mary her miraculous conception.

Q. Was Our Lord obliged to receive circumcision?

A. He was not. The law of circumcision was made for bondsmen and sinners, and as Christ was the Son of God, the master of the law, holiness itself, He was not under the law. We should admire the great example of humility which Jesus Christ here gives us. As in His birth He appeared to us as man, He wished at His circumcision to appear as a sinner.

Q. But if He was not subject to the law of circumcision, why subject Himself to it?

A. St. Thomas gives seven reasons for this, collected from the Fathers and Doctors of the Church. First, He willed to subject Himself to circumcision to prepare a proof against the heresies of the Manichians, the Apollonarists, and the Valentinians. The Manichians taught that the body of Christ was an apparition, not a real, material body; the Apollonarists held that His body was of the same substance as the Divinity—consubstantial with it; the Valentinians taught that the Divine Word brought His body from heaven. The act of circumcision proved that the body of Our Lord was a real, material body, subject to suffering and of the same material as ours, and thus the teachings of these heretics were disproved.

Q. What are the other reasons given by St. Thomas?

A. Besides that just given, Christ desired to be circumcised, first, to approve the rite of circumcision instituted by God in the covenant with Abraham; second, to prove to the world that He was descended from that patriarch to whom circumcision was exclusively commanded and from whom should descend the Saviour; third, to take from the Jews every pretext to reject Him as a stranger; fourth, to teach us by His example obedience to the laws; fifth, not to reject that remedy which until then was used to cleanse from sin; and lastly, to free us from that legal burden by substituting Himself for us all.

Q. Why was the Child called Jesus?

A. Because this name came from God by the mouth of the Archangel Gabriel, who was sent to the most holy Virgin and St. Joseph; and also because the name Jesus was the only one proper to Him Who had come to save the human race from eternal death, to reconcile men to God and open to them the gates of eternal life. *Jesus* signifies *saviour*.

Q. What is to be said in praise of this name?

A. It is the most precious balm to the Christian believer. St. Bernard calls it the oil that illuminates, that soothes and cures every wound. The name of Jesus illuminates the whole world as with oil; as oil it has nourished numbers and will always nourish pious souls; and as oil it heals all spiritual plagues, so that, in the words of St. Peter, in this name alone we can hope to obtain eternal life.

Q. How can it be said that the name of Jesus illuminates the whole world?

A. Before the name of Jesus was announced to the world the whole human race was in universal darkness. At its announcement the world learned to know God, to know the heavenly truths hitherto unknown to human philosophy, and to know the way to lead a just and holy life before God and men.

Q. How can it be said that the name of Jesus nourishes the just soul?

A. Nothing that is earthly can satisfy the soul of man. No matter how great his possessions, he can never be contented. But the just soul finds all in Jesus Christ. The intellect, the will, and the heart find in this name satiety, sweetness, and happiness. Be holy and you will experience the force, the value, and the truth of these words.

Q. How is the name of Jesus the balm of salvation?

A. As the lame man in the porch of the temple was cured by that name, so the soul that invokes it will be healed; the sinner, the weak, the doubting, and the afflicted, if they invoke the name of Jesus with faith and love, will find relief, and pass from death to life.

Q. What do we learn from the Child Jesus on this occasion?

A. If Jesus while yet so young wished to shed His

precious blood for love of us, we from our youth should consecrate to Him our sufferings, our afflictions, and our souls. If He, though not obliged to do so, subjected Himself to this most painful law, we also should make it a duty to obey willingly His Church and our spiritual and temporal superiors. And as His name is so great and powerful, we should learn to reverence it and to invoke it with confidence, that we may be enlightened, nourished, and freed from all our spiritual miseries.

FEAST OF THE EPIPHANY.

Gospel: St. Matthew ii. 1-12.

"WHEN Jesus therefore was born in Bethlehem of Juda, in the days of King Herod, behold, there came wise men from the East to Jerusalem, saying, Where is He that is born King of the Jews? For we have seen His star in the East, and we are come to adore Him. And King Herod, hearing this, was troubled, and all Jerusalem with him. And assembling together all the chief priests and the scribes of the people, he inquired of them where Christ should be born. But they said to him: In Bethlehem of Juda: for so it is written by the prophet: And thou, Bethlehem, the land of Juda, art not the least among the princes of Juda: for out of thee shall come forth the captain that shall rule My people Israel. Then Herod privately calling the wise men learned diligently of them the time of the star which appeared to them, and sending them into Bethlehem, said: Go and diligently inquire after the Child: and when you have found Him, bring me word again, that I also may come and adore Him. Who, having heard the king, went their way: and behold, the star which they had seen in the East went before them, until it came and stood over where the Child was. And seeing the star they rejoiced with exceeding great joy. And entering into the house, they found the Child with Mary His Mother; and falling down they adored Him: and opening their treasures, they offered Him gifts, gold, frankincense, and myrrh. And having received an answer in sleep that they should not return to Herod, they went back another way into their own country."

Q. Who was this Herod under whose government Christ was born?

A. He was the oldest son of Antipater, the Idumian from the city of Ascalon, who was appointed king of the Jews by the Roman Senate at the recommendation of Mark Antony. He was the father of Herod Antipas, who ordered the beheading of St. John the Baptist, and grandfather of Herod Agrippa, who caused St. James to be put to death and the same who imprisoned St. Peter. St. Matthew informs us that Herod ruled in the time of the birth of Christ, fulfilling the prophecy of Jacob, who foretold the coming of Christ when the sceptre had passed into the hands of strangers. This prophecy was verified when the Roman Senate appointed Herod, of Idumian origin, king of the Jews.

Q. Who were these Magi of whom the Evangelist speaks?

A. They were men distinguished for their knowledge, particularly of astronomy, and according to some Fathers and Doctors they were petty kings of the East who came, as was foretold in the seventy-first psalm, from Arabia and from Saba to offer their gifts and adoration to the Messias.

Q. In what way were they invited?

A. They saw the star which according to prophetic prediction was to appear when the promised Saviour was born, and by the interior operation of grace they recognized it as the sign of His birth and hastened to follow its course. According to the opinion of the Fathers, they were the first of the Gentiles who were called to enter into the Church of Christ.

Q. What is worthy of remark in the conduct of the Magi?

A. We must admire their promptness in corresponding to the invitation of grace. Immediately on the appearance of the star they, giving no heed to the suggestions of human prudence, the difficulties of the way, and the uncertainties of success, left their homes and set out in search of the Child; and while thus seeking in obedience to the voice of heaven, they teach us with what disregard of human interests, with what solicitude and courage, we should always follow divine inspiration and the call of heaven.

Q. But why were the Magi directed to Jerusalem?

A. We must here remember that a prophet had called Jerusalem the queen of the world and the joy of all the earth. In Jerusalem alone was the temple dedicated to the true God; to Jerusalem came worshippers from all parts of the world; there were preserved the holy books, and there were found the great teachers of the law. For this reason the Magi directed their steps to the capital of the nation, reasonably hoping to find there a most certain guide who could conduct them to the desired place. We learn from this to have recourse to those who by reason of their sacred character, office, learning, and prudence may direct our steps when we feel impelled by some interior call of heaven.

Q. What are we to think of the question of the Magi when in Jerusalem in reference to the new-born King of the Jews?

A. Their questionings left without excuse the people of Jerusalem who did not recognize and strive to know the Saviour. The coming of the Magi and their seeking for the new-born King of the Jews should have attracted the attention of all in the city, and the answers which the Doctors of the Law, after consulting the books of the prophets, gave to them and to Herod, by whom they were consulted, should have attracted the attention of every citizen to what had happened in full conformity with the expectations of their fathers, with the desires of the people, and with the circumstances in which all the prophecies culminated. It would be unfortunate for us if we, like the Jews, should attribute to accident or fate that which is God's work.

Q. What are we to say of the promise of Herod?

A. The cries of the children brutally slaughtered by his command give the answer. His zealous devotion to the new-born King of the Jews was hypocritically assumed in order to deceive the Magi and get the divine Infant into his power that he might put Him to death. His deceit failing of its object, he commanded all the male infants to be put to death that in the general slaughter the infant Jesus might be included. Alas! not all those who make a show of zeal for the truth, justice, and glory of the Eternal Father are lovers of Jesus Christ.

Q. What is to be said of the Magi who, after departing from Jerusalem, again saw the star which had led them from the East?

A. We should comfort ourselves with the reflection that when, like the Magi, we sincerely seek to know the divine will, and seek in the proper manner by consulting learned and enlightened teachers, we will be led to the desired end. God is faithful. Let us submit ourselves to His guidance and He will send us His light to direct us.

Q. How did the Magi recognize the infant Messias Whom they sought?

A. From the words of the Sacred Text it is to be inferred that the star stopped over the place where the Child Jesus reposed, and this wonderful event attracted the attention of the Magi and caused them to enter. It is not difficult to imagine the impression the presence of the God-man made on them and the grace it wrought in them. He Who when grown up knew how to call His apostles after Him, could as a child make Himself known to the Magi, and make them His worshippers.

Q. What did the Magi offer Him, and with what intention?

A. The Gospel tells us they offered Him gold, frankincense, and myrrh. By the gold, says St. Gregory, they recognized Him as king, by the incense they acknowledged Him as God, and by the myrrh they indicated His human nature. They, says St. Leo, proclaimed by the nature of their gifts the faith that was in their hearts, and with full knowledge they venerated in His person two natures, the divine and human of Jesus Christ.

Q. What are we to learn from this Gospel?

A. We should learn to recognize in the Magi the first-fruits of our vocation to the faith, and to thank God that we have been made Christians. We should learn also to follow the divine call and to offer to Jesus Christ the gold of charity, the incense of prayer, and the myrrh of holy mortification and Christian penance.

FIRST SUNDAY AFTER EPIPHANY.

Gospel: St. Luke ii. 42–52.

"AND when Jesus was twelve years old, they went up to Jerusalem, according to the custom of the feast. And having fulfilled the days, when they returned, the Child Jesus remained in Jerusalem, and His parents knew it not. And thinking that He was in the company, they came a day's journey and sought Him among their kinsfolk and acquaintance; and not finding Him, they returned into Jerusalem seeking Him. And it came to pass that after three days they found Him in the temple, sitting in the midst of the doctors, hearing them and asking questions. And all that heard Him were astonished at His wisdom and His answers. And seeing Him, they wondered. And His Mother said to Him: Son, why hast thou done so to us: Behold, Thy father and I have sought Thee sorrowing. And He said to them: How is it that you sought Me? Did you not know that I must be about My Father's business? And they understood not the word that He spoke unto them. And He went down with them, and came to Nazareth, and was subject to them. And His Mother kept all these words in her heart. And Jesus advanced in wisdom, and age, and grace with God and men."

Q. What does St. Luke tell us here?

A. He tells us that Our Lord at the age of twelve

years went with His holy Mother and St. Joseph to Jerusalem to be present at the festival, which was solemnized for seven days, in the Temple, and the feast of the Pasch or Passover; that these days being over, He was lost from their sight and remained in Jerusalem in the Temple while they set out for their home believing that He was in the company of His relatives.

Q. Were Mary and Joseph inattentive or negligent on this occasion?

A. Certainly not. But God had thus disposed it, and the greatest human vigilance cannot avail against the dispositions of divine Providence.

Q. What did they do after having lost Jesus?

A. They were in great affliction, and hastened to seek for Him among their friends and relatives, and not finding Him, they returned to Jerusalem, hoping to find Him there.

Q. What should the just learn from the afflictions of Mary and Joseph?

A. They should learn that even souls most dear to God are not exempt from trials and tribulations, and that God sometimes withdraws Himself from them in despondency, fear, and temptations for the sole purpose of increasing their virtue, their merit, and their glory in heaven.

Q. And what may sinners learn from these holy persons?

A. They should learn what ought to be the sentiments of their own hearts when they have lost God by their sins; how eagerly they should seek to find Him by repentance, and that they should have recourse to the friends of God, the saints, to obtain the graces necessary for a true conversion.

Q. What does Jesus teach us by the reply to His Mother?

A. He teaches us that when there is a question of the glory of God, the interests of religion, or the duties of conscience, we should disregard all human considerations.

Q. Where did Jesus Christ go after leaving Jerusalem on this occasion?

A. He went with the Blessed Virgin and St. Joseph to the village of Nazareth in the tribe of Zabulon, where they dwelt.

Q. How far is Nazareth from Jerusalem?

A. About seventy miles. From this we may know the inconveniences these holy persons underwent in order to be present at the solemnities in Jerusalem. In view of this, how culpable are those who for slight cause, or no cause at all, absent themselves from divine service on Sundays and holydays.

Q. What did Jesus Christ do in the house of Joseph?

A. He lived poor and unknown in submission and obedience to His foster-father and to Mary His Mother, and the Scriptures tell us that He grew in wisdom and grace before God and man.

Q. What should we learn from this?

A. We should learn that if Jesus Christ, King of kings and Lord of lords, did not refuse to obey Mary and Joseph, we should not refuse to obey humbly and voluntarily our parents, superiors, and all who are charged with our care and education. What a consolation to think when obeying that we imitate Jesus

Christ, Who by His submission to Mary and Joseph sanctified and made obedience meritorious.

Q. Is there anything more to be said on this Gospel?

A. Yes. It is stated that Jesus increased in age, in wisdom, and in grace. From this we should learn that we also as we advance in years should increase in the knowledge of religion, in Christian virtue, and in the observance of the duties of our state in life. As Jesus increased in grace before men and in merit before God, so we as we grow older should make ourselves beloved of men by our charity, and beloved of God by abounding in merit, by the exercises of piety, and above all by frequenting the holy sacraments.

SECOND SUNDAY AFTER EPIPHANY.

Gospel: St. John ii. 1-11.

AT that time: " There was a marriage in Cana of Galilee: and the Mother of Jesus was there. And Jesus also was invited, and His disciples, to the marriage. And the wine failing, the Mother of Jesus saith to Him: They have no wine. And Jesus saith to her: Woman, what is that to Me and to thee? My hour is not yet come. His Mother saith to the waiters: Whatsoever He shall say to you, do ye. Now there were set there six water-pots of stone, according to the manner of the purifying of the Jews, containing two or three measures apiece. Jesus saith to them: Fill the water-pots with water. And they filled them up to the brim. And Jesus saith to them: Draw out now and carry to the chief steward of the feast. And they carried it. And when the chief steward had tasted the water made wine, and knew not whence it was, but the waiters knew who had drawn the water: the chief steward calleth the bridegroom, and saith to him: Every man at first setteth forth good wine, and when men have well drank, then that which is worse: but thou hast kept the good wine until now. This beginning of miracles did Jesus in Cana of Galilee, and He manifested His glory, and His disciples believed in Him."

Q. Is it not strange that Jesus and Mary were invited to a wedding-feast?

A. No. Because it is said that the husband was Simon, the son of Cleophas the brother of St. Joseph and therefore nephew of the Blessed Virgin and cousin, according to law, of Jesus Christ. Besides, at that feast there were no improprieties or over-indulgence, which so often dishonors the tables of many Christians, to be feared. And lastly, Jesus Christ, as St. John Chrysostom tells us, wished to give to the world a useful lesson.

Q. What was this lesson?

A. When at the wedding Jesus took occasion to manifest His divine power by which those present were led to recognize in Him the expected Messias. Besides, He prepared a condemnation of those heretics who taught that matrimony was the work of the devil. And lastly, He wished to teach us that we should not refuse to contribute, when we are able, to the innocent enjoyment of our friends, for in this way the bond of peace and Christian friendship is preserved.

Q. Why did Mary take such great interest when she knew that there was no more wine?

A. St. Bernard tells us she is truly the Mother of mercy. She foresaw and felt the shame and confusion of the poor husband and wife when the wine would give out before the feast was over. In her goodness, tenderness, and charity she begged Jesus to provide it and relieve them from humiliation by a miracle. Oh, if all Christians had equal solicitude to spare their neighbors shame and confusion! But too frequently the confusion of others is a triumph and a joy to many egotists who are always talking about charity without knowing what it is.

Q. Why then did Jesus reply that His hour had not yet come?

A. Up to this time, says St. John Chrysostom, only the Blessed Virgin had noticed the failure of the wine, and if He had immediately worked the miracle requested of Him, she alone and no others would have known and attested it. It was not yet time for such a great work. It was necessary to wait till all were aware that the wine had given out, so that all would be witnesses of the miracle and recognize the omnipotence and divinity of Jesus Christ. It was perhaps for this reason also that Mary said to the servants: Do whatsoever He commands you.

Q. Could not Jesus have produced the wine in some other manner?

A. No doubt He could have done so, but it pleased Him, says St. Chrysostom, to make use of the work of the servants that they might see the prodigy wrought and testify to the truth of the miracle by which the divinity of our Redeemer was made manifest.

Q. Is there anything to observe about this miracle?

A. We should observe that Jesus Christ by this miracle prepared the way for that still greater miracle which He was to work in the institution of the Most

Holy Sacrament, by showing that as He was able to convert insipid water into generous wine He could also convert bread and wine into His own body and blood.

Q. Did Jesus wish to teach us anything else by this miracle?

A. He wished to teach us that as water serves in the order of nature to purify the body, so His precious blood, symbolized by the wine, sanctifies the soul in the order of grace.

Q. Did not the water also symbolize the human race?

A. Yes, as the water was transformed by the power of Jesus Christ into delicious wine, so the human race, devoid of merit and valueless in itself, became sweetened and precious before God by the grace, merits, and blood of Our Saviour.

Q. What are we to learn from the married couple in this day's Gospel?

A. We should learn to conduct ourselves at our tables and nuptials as if Jesus were invited and present by His grace. Jesus Christ will bless the nuptials of those who are led by a right motive and not by caprice, interest, and passion; and He will bless our tables when sobriety, modesty, and the fear of God are present.

Q. What are we to learn from the intervention of Mary?

A. If the Blessed Virgin felt such compassion for that poor couple in a temporal matter, how much may we not hope from her when the object is spiritual and in favor of our souls. If unasked she showed such an interest in them as to ask her Son to work a miracle, what will she not do for us when we confide in her tenderness and invoke her by the name of mother?

Q. Is there anything further to learn?

A. As Jesus immediately complied with the request of Mary, how promptly will He not grant us every grace when His most Blessed Mother speaks in our behalf?

Q. In what way can we interest Mary in our favor?

A. By doing faithfully all that Jesus Christ commands us to do; then by imitating her holy virtues, particularly her humility, mercy, modesty, charity towards our neighbor and her zeal for the glory of God, and finally by having for her a sincere and filial devotion, and by invoking her frequently as a tender mother.

THIRD SUNDAY AFTER EPIPHANY.

Gospel: St. Matthew viii. 1-13.

AT that time: "When Jesus was come down from the mountain, great multitudes followed Him. And behold a leper came and adored Him, saying: Lord, if Thou wilt, Thou canst make me clean. And Jesus stretching forth His hand, touched him, saying: I will. Be thou made clean. And forthwith his leprosy was cleansed. And Jesus saith to him: See thou tell no man: but go, show thyself to the priest, and offer the gift which Moses commanded for a testimony unto them. And when He had entered into Capharnaum there came to Him a centurion, beseeching Him, and saying: Lord, my servant lieth at home sick of the palsy, and is grievously tormented. And Jesus saith to him: I will come and heal him. And the centurion making answer said: Lord, I am not worthy that thou shouldst enter under my roof: but only say the word, and my servant shall be healed. For I also am a man subject to authority, having under me soldiers; and I say to this man Go, and he goeth; and to another Come, and he cometh; and to my servant Do this, and he doeth it. And Jesus hearing this, marvelled, and said to them that followed Him: Amen I say to you, I have not found so great faith in Israel. And I say unto you that many shall come from the East and the West, and shall sit down with Abraham, and Isaac, and Jacob in the kingdom of heaven: but the children of the kingdom shall be cast out into the exterior darkness: there shall be weeping and gnashing of teeth. And Jesus said to the centurion: Go, and as thou hast believed so be it done to thee. And the servant was healed at the same hour."

Q. Of whom was this leper a figure?

A. This man who was afflicted with the leprosy and healed by the Redeemer was an image of man corrupted by sin and by means of penance cured by the powerful grace of Jesus Christ.

Q. How do you explain the prostration which he made and his words: Lord, if thou wilt Thou canst make me clean?

A. This man by his adoration teaches us with what humility, faith, and abasement the truly contrite sinner should present himself before God; and by his words he gives us an example of the great confidence and submission to the divine will with which penitents should implore the healing of their souls and beg to be freed from temptations.

Q. Can it be said that God does with sinners as He did with the leper?

A. He does so in a spiritual manner. God reaches forth His hand and touches the sinner when in His mercy He arouses him, calls him, and softens his heart, however hardened by sin. He says "I will" when by His powerful grace He enables him to break his chains. He says "Be thou healed" when He applies the merits of Jesus Christ to his soul by the ministry of the priest, and frees him from the leprosy of sin.

Q. Why did Jesus command the leper not to make this miracle known?

A. This is an important lesson to the ministers of the sanctuary and to all Christians, that they should, according to their ability, do all the good possible in the Church and for the salvation of their fellow-men without glorifying themselves and without making it known in order to gain praise or reward.

Q. What is to be said about the command to show himself to the priest and to offer the gifts prescribed by the law?

A. It was prescribed in the law that lepers when cured should present themselves to the priests that they might be declared free from legal uncleanness, and on such occasions they were required to make an offering. If Our Lord had dispensed the leper from this custom He would have without reason disparaged the Mosaic Law and caused surprise and scandal. On this account He commanded the leper to comply with the law and at the same time taught all those who assist sinners that they should not depart from the ordinary discipline, that they should avoid novelty, and oblige the penitent to conform to all laws regarding reparation of scandal and injury to the interests or reputation of others. Penitents should submit with docility, as the leper did, to the commands of the ministers of God, who should insist on the observance of the law, however onerous it may be.

Q. Who was the centurion who presented himself to Our Lord?

A. He was a Roman soldier, a captain of a hundred men who garrisoned the town of Capharnaum. There are some who think that this was the same Cornelius who, warned by an angel, as we read in the Acts of the Apostles, sent for St. Peter to instruct him in the faith and baptize him; and also that he might have been the father of that other centurion who was in command at the crucifixion of Christ, and who exclaimed: Truly, this Jesus was the Son of God.

Q. Of what was the paralysis of the centurion's servant an image?

A. It was an image of the state of a soul deprived of the grace of God. Those who saw that servant saw an unhappy man, trembling all over, unable to direct his steps or perform any act, subject to fits, miserable and dying. Now, the soul without the grace of God is in a like condition. It cannot direct its steps on account of the shocks of the passions; it can do nothing good; it yields to temptation, is deprived of true comfort, and is ever suspended over the sepulchre of eternal death. Oh, let us pray, and pray continually to God that we may never be deprived of the help of His grace.

Q. What may we learn from this centurion?

A. He is to be admired for his charity to his servant and for his great humility in confessing his unworthiness to receive Jesus Christ into his house. Employers should learn of him that charity which they should have for those under them. And all Christians should learn to recognize themselves as unworthy of the favors which God is pleased to confer upon them through His merciful kindness and not through any merit of their own. Lastly, let us reflect that the Church takes so great account of the words of the centurion that she deems them worthy to be repeated three times when we are about to receive Jesus Christ into our hearts in the holy Communion.

Q. And what are we to learn from the words of Christ, "I will come and heal him"?

A. These words should inspire us with consoling hope and convince us that God is prompt in granting His mercy when we ask His assistance with the faith, confidence, and humility of the centurion.

Q. Why did Jesus show surprise at the faith of the centurion?

A. Our Lord knew well the excellent dispositions of the centurion before he spoke, but He wished to manifest His surprise for His own wise purposes. He desired to show the mercy of His Eternal Father, Who gave the grace of such great faith and humility to a man educated in the army and among the Gentiles. He wished to call the attention of the Jews to their blindness in being so slow to recognize that Messias Whom, by reason of the prophecies and of the miracles worked by Him, they should have been the first to recognize. He wished to give a reproof to those Christians who with the many means of salvation at their disposal belie their faith by their works and place themselves out of the way of salvation.

Q. What did Jesus intend when He said that many

would come from the East and from the West to repose in the bosom of Abraham, and that the children of the kingdom would be cast out and condemned to darkness?

A. By these words He foretold that the Gentiles would embrace the faith and enter into the Church, while the Jews, the first called, would, through their incredulity and obstinacy, be excluded and condemned. He shows us also that though living in the bosom of the Church we are not certain of dying therein, for if we fail in Christian perseverance we shall be excluded from the kingdom of heaven. Lastly, He has warned us to be as persevering in the faith as Abraham, as obedient unto death as Isaac, and as full of confidence as Jacob, in the hope of the happiness of heaven.

FOURTH SUNDAY AFTER EPIPHANY.

Gospel: St. Matthew viii. 23–27.

AT that time: "When He entered into the boat His disciples followed Him: And behold a great tempest arose in the sea, so that the ship was covered with waves, but He was asleep. And His disciples came to Him, and awaked Him, saying: Lord, save us, we perish. And Jesus saith to them: Why are you fearful, O ye of little faith? Then rising up, He commanded the winds and the sea, and there came a great calm. But the men wondered, saying: What manner of man is this, for the winds and the sea obey Him?"

Q. What does this ship into which Christ entered represent?

A. It represents holy Church placed in the midst

of the vicissitudes of the world like a ship in mid-ocean. Jesus Christ, on account of His promise, is ever found with His disciples in the Catholic Church as He was with His apostles in the ship on the Sea of Galilee. This should be a great consolation to us. He who keeps his mind fixed on this great truth sees what takes place in the Church in a very different light from that in which it is seen by the outside world.

Q. Does this ship represent only the Church?

A. It also symbolizes a human soul in which Jesus Christ is present by His grace. This soul is like a ship amid the angry waves; every passion threatens a storm, every pleasure a rock, and the whole course of life is a sea full of dangers through which it must pass. If this soul can keep Jesus Christ with it, the winds will cease, the tempest abate, the dangers vanish, tranquillity prevail, and it will come safe, laden with merit, to the harbor of Eternal Life.

Q. What do the winds and tempest signify in reference to the just soul?

A. To the just soul the winds and tempest are temptations, fears, anxieties, and tribulations of every kind, which God frequently permits souls dear to Him to undergo. The Antonys, the Hilarions, the Teresas, the Magdalens di Pazzi, and the Chantals have experienced this great truth to their greater glory and for the consolation of all Christians.

Q. What means the sleep of Christ?

A. It means that God, in His inscrutable ways, does not always stop in their beginning the storms that rise up against the Church or allay the afflictions of just souls, but permits rather that they increase and become furious while He seems to sleep, to show us the necessity of having recourse to Him, and that we may win, by our own strength assisted by His grace, a more glorious crown in heaven. He permits the storm to acquire its full strength because His power is more manifest when at the proper time He raises His omnipotent hand and produces the unlooked-for calm.

Q. What do we learn from the apostles who hastened to awake Christ?

A. We learn that in public as well as private dangers, in calamities of Church or State as well as in dangers to our souls, we should invoke Him with confidence as the apostles did, and with hearts full of love and free from the stain of sin.

Q. Why did Jesus Christ reprove the apostles for awaking Him?

A. He did not reprove them for awaking Him, but because they were wanting in faith and feared that they were about to perish, although He was so near. Those who fear should remember His words and learn to confide in that God Who sometimes appears to sleep, but Who is never far away, that God Who protects them with the tenderness of a father and leads them that they may not fall.

Q. Is there nothing more to be observed?

A. Jesus Christ, notwithstanding the little faith of the apostles, immediately calmed the storm; and while admiring His infinite goodness we see how a prayer, imperfect in the beginning, can lead us to the treasures of divine mercy. Let every sinner have recourse to Jesus Christ, and if not immediately, he will at least in a short time see the tempest cease and find peace.

Q. What means "after the storm there came a great calm"?

A. From this we learn that God, the inexhaustible fountain of goodness, does not leave His children long in affliction, and that after the storm He brings the calm; when we are in affliction we must expect consolation. Remain near Jesus, as the apostles did, and the storms of this life will make all the more sweet the tranquillity which we hope for in Paradise.

FIFTH SUNDAY AFTER EPIPHANY.

Gospel: St. Matthew xiii. 24–30.

AT that time: Jesus spoke this parable to the multitude, saying: " The kingdom of heaven is likened to a man that sowed good seed in his field; but while men were asleep his enemy came and oversowed cockle among the wheat, and went his way. And when the blade was sprung up, and had brought forth fruit, then appeared also the cockle. And the servants of the good man of the house coming said to him: Sir, didst thou not sow good seed in thy field? Whence then hath it cockle? And he said to them: An enemy hath done this. And the servants said to him: Wilt thou that we go and gather it up? And he said: No: lest perhaps gathering up the cockle you root up the wheat also together with it. Suffer both to grow until the harvest, and in the time of the harvest I will say to the reapers: Gather up first the cockle, and bind it into bundles to burn, but the wheat gather ye into my barn."

Q. Who is this man who sowed the good seed?

A. Jesus Christ, in the continuation of the discourse explaining the parable to the apostles, tells us that the sower is the Son of God, that is, Himself.

Q. What is the field in which the good seed is sown?

A. It is the whole world, in which, on every side, was sown by the apostles and their successors the seed of the gospel, that is, the doctrine of Jesus Christ.

Q. What is meant by the good seed?

A. At first view it might be said that the good seed is the word of God, but according to the explanation of the Divine Master we are to understand by the good seed the effect rather than the cause, and therefore the good seed signifies the effect of the word of God, that is, the good Christians produced by the preaching of the apostles and their successors, the bishops, assisted by the priests, who teach the people in their name.

Q. What does the cockle represent?

A. It represents sinners, heretics, teachers of perverse doctrines, in a word—all bad Christians.

Q. Who is the enemy that sowed the cockle?

A. The enemy that sowed the cockle is the devil, who incites sinners to evil, and all those who make themselves ministers of iniquity by scandals and perverse teachings.

Q. Who are meant by those that by sleeping gave opportunity to the enemy to sow cockle?

A. Some think their sleep signifies the death of the apostles; but in those who by sleeping gave opportunity to the devil to sow the cockle we can recognize those ministers of the sanctuary who, negligent in the performance of their duties and wanting in vigilance and zeal, permit evil customs and ignorance to destroy the vineyard of Christ.

Q. Do those who sleep represent these only?

A. Those who sleep and give the devil time to sow cockle represent also those parents, heads of communities, and teachers who, devoid of the necessary solicitude and proper attention, leave those under them exposed to danger, and permit evil customs and disorders to be introduced into the home, the schools, and other places of education.

Q. Who are those servants who point out and wish to uproot the cockle?

A. Some think these servants represent those overzealous persons who wish to tolerate neither sinners nor defects in the world. Others see in these servants the angels of the Lord, ministers of His wrath, instruments of His vengeance, death, public calamities, and all those disasters that would in a short time exterminate sinners if God in His infinite mercy did not prevent them.

Q. Does God, according to this Gospel, spare the sinner for the sake of the just?

A. Pestilence, war, and misfortunes of every kind spare princes and nations on account of the just souls who would suffer thereby. Thus the dissolute Sodom and Gomorrha would have been spared if only ten just men, like Lot, could have been found in them, as God promised to Abraham.

Q. But why does God permit sinners to continue in the world, or the mysterious cockle to increase together with the good wheat?

A. God does this, says St. Augustine, to give time to sinners to be converted, and also to give occasion to the just to exercise patience and to render themselves perfect in the midst of those who persecute them and who by their scandals tempt them to sin.

Q. What is the harvest time in which the cockle will be separated from the good wheat?

A. The harvest time is the last day of the world, in which good Christians will be separated from the wicked; when the just will be placed on the right hand and the impious on the left of Jesus Christ, Who will be the Judge.

Q. Who will make this separation?

A. The angels of the Lord will make it, as Christ has already told us. Immediately on the resurrection of the flesh the angels will distinguish the just from the impious and separate them.

Q. And will the angels favor no one?

A. They will favor no one. Relationship, nobility, honors, titles, talents, learning, dress, sword, mitre, sceptre will on that day protect no one. The just will be on the right hand, the wicked on the left, and every one will be judged according to his works.

Q. What is the barn into which the wheat will be gathered, and what the place into which the cockle will be cast?

A. The wheat, that is, the just, will be gathered together in the paradise of God, and the cockle, that is, the wicked, will be cast into hell for all eternity.

Q. What should we learn from this parable?

A. We should learn three things. First, to be vigilant that the devil may not sow cockle in our hearts or in the hearts of those under our care. Second, to console and sympathize with poor sinners. Third, to endeavor to make ourselves wheat for paradise and not cockle for eternal fire.

SIXTH SUNDAY AFTER EPIPHANY.

Gospel: St. Matthew xiii. 31-35.

AT that time, Jesus spoke this parable to the multitudes, saying: "The kingdom of heaven is like to a grain of mustard seed, which a man took and sowed in his field; which is the least indeed of all seeds, but when it is grown up it is greater than all herbs, and becometh a tree, so that the birds of the air come and dwell in the branches thereof. Another parable He spoke to them: The kingdom of heaven is like to leaven, which a woman took and hid in three measures of meal, until the whole was leavened. All these things Jesus spoke in parables to the multitudes: and without parables He did not speak to them: that it might be fulfilled which was spoken by the prophet, saying: I will open My mouth in parables, I will utter things hidden from the foundation of the world."

Q. What is meant by the grain of mustard seed?

A. St. Hilary tells us that by the grain of mustard seed Our Lord Jesus Christ Himself is meant.

Q. How is it a figure of Christ?

A. By its littleness, its increase, and its virtues.

Q. How is it a figure of Christ by its littleness?

A. Though the grain of mustard seed is capable of great development, before it is put in the ground it is among the smallest of seeds. So Jesus Christ, though He is great, strong, and glorious by His divinity, and though He is to receive the adoration of the whole world on account of His glorious resurrection, yet He belittled, humiliated, annihilated Himself so as to appear weak, afflicted of God, a worm and not a man, the opprobrium of the Gentiles, and a stumbling-block to the multitude.

Q. How is Jesus Christ represented by the increase of the mustard seed?

A. As the little seed, in its development, rises from the earth, grows large and strong, and affords shelter and refuge to the beasts and birds, so Jesus Christ, rising and going forth from the sepulchre, triumphed in the midst of human generations and received under the shadow of His cross not only the ignorant and the lowly but also the wise and the great; not only sinners who came to take refuge at His feet, but also the just, who, flying as the eagle on high, find in Him an asylum, strength and nourishment, in the difficult way of evangelical perfection.

Q. How is Jesus Christ represented by the virtues of the mustard seed?

A. This seed is regarded as a vigorous excitant, an agreeable condiment, and an efficacious medicine. In like manner, Jesus Christ by His doctrines aroused the people from the lethargy of their passions; by His example He made sweet and light all duties however painful or difficult, and by His grace He healed all our infirmities and preserved the health and life of our souls.

Q. Is not the Church also symbolized by the mustard seed?

A. Yes, the Church is also indicated by the words of Christ. The Church in the beginning was composed of but few persons, the apostles, the disciples, and five hundred others who, as St. Peter tells us, had seen the Redeemer after His resurrection. But this Church, so small at its birth, spread with wonderful rapidity throughout the whole world, and in her bosom men found comfort, repose, and consolation.

Q. And what means the parable of the woman who hid the leaven in the three measures of meal till all was fermented?

A. According to St. Augustine, the woman is a figure of the Church, the leaven is the preaching of the apostles, and the fermentation is that change of mind, will, and affections which is produced in men by the preaching of the gospel.

Q. Can we not also learn something from this parable in regard to morals?

A. Yes. The grain of mustard, which develops into a plant and gives refuge and shelter to bird and beast, teaches us how great an increase a little virtue is capable of when kept and nourished in the heart by a faithful compliance with grace. And the little leaven, which sours the meal, shows the ruin which one single vice may produce in the body and mind of youth when not repressed in the beginning.

Q. But why did Jesus Christ speak to the multitude in parables?

A. This way of speaking practised by Our Redeemer affords a singular proof of His divine mission. The Royal Prophet had said, in the seventy-seventh psalm, that the coming Christ would speak in parables, and by them reveal truths hidden from the eyes of the world; and therefore the Divine Teacher, even in this particular, gave a sign by which He could be recognized when He taught the multitude in parables.

Q. In view of all this, what should we do?

A. In the first place, we should understand that the triumphs of the gospel are not the work of chance or of men, but of God, Who prepared for it and accomplished it. In the second place, we should rejoice that we are now no longer instructed by shadows and figures not always easily understood, but in a manner clear and evident. In conclusion, we should see to it that the germs of faith should grow vigorously in our intellect, engraft themselves on our will, bloom in the affections of our heart, and bring forth the fruit of good works.

SEPTUAGESIMA SUNDAY.

Gospel: St. Matthew xx. 1–16.

AT that time, Jesus said to His disciples this parable: "The kingdom of heaven is like to a householder, who went early in the morning to hire laborers into his vineyard. And having agreed with the laborers for a penny a day, he sent them into his vineyard. And going out about the third hour he saw others standing in the market-place idle, and he said to them: Go you also into my vineyard, and I will give you what shall be just. And they went their way. And again he went out about the sixth and the ninth hour, and did in like manner. But about the eleventh hour he went out and found others standing, and he saith to them: Why stand you here all the day idle? They say to him: Because no man hath hired us. He saith to them: Go you also into my vineyard. And when evening was come the lord of the vineyard saith to his steward: Call the laborers and pay them their hire, beginning from the last even to the first. When therefore they were come that came about the eleventh hour they received every man a penny. But when the first also came, they thought that they should receive more: and they also received every man a penny. And receiving it they murmured against the master of the house, saying: These last have worked but one hour, and thou hast made them equal to us, that have borne the burden of the day and the heats. But he answering said to one of them: Friend, I do thee no wrong: didst thou not agree with me for a penny? Take what is thine, and go thy way: I will also give to this last even as to thee. Or, is it not lawful for me to do what I will? Is thy eye evil because I am good? So shall the last be first, and the first, last; for many are called, but few chosen."

Q. What of this householder, his vineyard, and the wages?

A. In the householder we recognize God; in the vineyard the Fathers recognize the Church of Jesus Christ; and in the wages they see the glories of paradise promised as a reward to all those who have worked in the divine service, that is, in the profession and practice of the gospel.

Q. How do you explain the parable?

A. It can be explained in two ways. It may be applied to men in general or to each Christian in particular.

Q. How is it applied to all in general?

A. The early morning signifies the time from Adam to Noe; the third hour represents the time from Abraham to Moses; the ninth hour the time from Moses to Christ; the eleventh hour the time from Christ to the end of the world; and the evening is the great day of judgment.

Q. If it be thus, how is it explained?

A. From the beginning of the world, that is, the morning, the third, sixth, and ninth hours, God, by the voice and example of the patriarchs, by the written law, and by the words of the prophets, called men, particularly the Hebrews, to believe in Christ and hope for His coming, and to unite themselves to Him by holiness of life. At the eleventh hour, by the preaching of Christ and of His apostles and their successors, God has called, calls, and will continue to call men to enter into the Catholic Church and become living members of the mystical body of Jesus Christ and to serve Him faithfully by observing His holy laws. In the evening, that is, on the day of judgment, all those who will have belonged to the Church of Christ, who will have entered the Church—the vineyard—in the early morning, at the third, sixth, ninth, or eleventh hour, will receive without distinction, in reward of their labors, eternal life and the glory of Paradise.

Q. How is the parable applied to each Christian in particular?

A. The early morning is childhood; the third hour, youth; the sixth hour, manhood; the ninth hour, old age; the eleventh hour, the last days of life, the last sickness. By baptism, by the first development of reason, and by Christian instruction, we are called to work in the evangelical vineyard by faith and holiness of life. Many are called in youth, many in manhood, many in old age, and many at the end of life, after having gone in the way of sin and wandered in every field of iniquity. All those who have served God will receive as a reward the glories of paradise.

Q. But what service can we give God at the last hour?

A. A sincere repentance, an act of perfect charity, a lively desire, a firm purpose of serving faithfully if life be prolonged, will be accepted by a merciful God as service sufficient to merit eternal reward in the land of the living. It was in this way that the penitent thief heard the answer to his prayer: This day thou shalt be with Me in paradise.

Q. Can we then delay to work for God till the last hour?

A. No. To do this would be foolish and impious. God has no need of us, no obligation to call us. He may call us to-day; He may not call us to-morrow; and he who answers not His voice one day exposes himself to being rejected another day.

Q. Were the complaints of those laborers who worked all day reasonable?

A. No. If the householder wished to give to the last comers for the work of one hour as much as he had contracted to give to those who had worked all day, he was free to do so, because in so doing he did not diminish the wages due to them. He was just to them, while he was generous to the late comers.

Q. Are all then equally rewarded by God—those who are converted in their old age, or in their last hour, as those who have served God all their lives?

A. We cannot say so. God rewards generously as well those who are converted late as those who labored from the first hour, but we must consider that the service in the vineyard of the Lord is not measured solely by duration of time, but also by fervor, fidelity, right intention, and, above all, by the intensity of the love with which it is done. On this account a true penitent can surpass in a short time those who have been more or less inconstant and tepid during their whole life. Observe also that in heaven there are different crowns, and that while all enjoy the happiness of paradise, those who have served with greater merit are rewarded by God with a greater degree of glory.

Q. What is meant by the words: "The first shall be last and the last shall be first"?

A. The Jews were first called to enter the Church of Christ, but on account of their obstinacy they were excluded and are the last. The Gentiles, on the other hand, were the last called to the faith, but were the first to embrace it and enter the Church of Jesus Christ. We who are called to serve God from our infancy should be careful not to be the last in our old age.

Q. How do you explain these words: "Many are called, but few are chosen"?

A. Because there are many who by virtue of baptism enter into the vineyard to labor and gain eternal reward, but there are few who observe faithfully the holy law and who serve God with perseverance until death. Only the innocent and the truly penitent who have persevered to the last will be chosen. We must remember that without the grace of God we can do nothing toward our own salvation. Let us live in fear and humility; trust ourselves to the divine mercy; pray in the name of Jesus, and the terrible sentence will have no reference to us.

SEXAGESIMA SUNDAY.

Gospel: St. Luke viii. 4-15.

AT that time: "When a very great multitude was gathered together, and hastened out of the cities unto Him, He spoke by a similitude: A sower went out to sow his seed: and, as he sowed, some fell by the wayside and it was trodden down, and the fowls of the air devoured it. And other some fell upon a rock: and as soon as it was sprung up, it withered away, because it had no moisture. And other some fell among thorns, and the thorns growing up with it, choked it. And other some fell upon good ground, and sprung up and yielded fruit a hundred-fold. Saying these things He cried out: He that hath ears to hear, let him hear. And His disciples asked Him what this parable might be. To whom He said: To you it is given to know the mystery of the kingdom of God, but to the rest in parables: that seeing they may not see, and hearing they may not understand. Now this parable is this: The seed is the word of God. And they by the wayside are they that hear: then the devil cometh, and taketh the word out of their heart, lest believing they should be saved. Now they upon the rock are they who, when they hear, receive the word with joy: and these have no roots, who believe for a while, and in time of temptation fall away. And that which fell among thorns are they who have heard, and going their way, are choked with the cares and riches and pleasures of this life, and yield no fruit. But that on the good ground are they who in a good and perfect heart, hearing the word, keep it, and bring forth fruit in patience."

Q. What did Our Lord wish to teach by this parable?

A. He wished to say that of all those who came to see and hear Him comparatively few would profit by His divine teaching.

Q. What did He mean when He said, "He that hath ears to hear, let him hear"?

A. To believe in Jesus Christ, to hear His words and understand the significance of His wonderful works, the divine gift of grace is first of all necessary. Even St. Peter could not have recognized in Him the Son of the living God if it had not been revealed to him. Besides the divine grace there is also necessary a docile heart, a sincere mind, and an ardent desire to be enlightened in the things necessary for gaining eternal life. Now, among the multitude that collected about Our Lord to hear His words and witness His miracles there were but few who had these necessary conditions; there were, on the contrary, many who opposed Him and refused to yield to the many proofs He continually gave of His mission and His divine nature. When therefore He said, He that hath ears to hear, let him hear, He meant to say: He who is faithful to the grace he receives, and hears Me with a sincere mind and upright heart, will understand the meaning of My parables and the salutary significance of My words.

Q. How, then, could He say that He spoke in parables that they might not understand Him?

A. In reading St. Matthew these words are easily understood: they mean that in thus speaking Jesus Christ wished to say, not indeed that He spoke in parables that they might not understand Him, but that many, because of their bad motives and blind passions, saw the wonders worked by Him and heard

His words, but did not understand the meaning of His teaching. Observe that the merit of the Christian depends on faith; that in view of this fact Christ does not force the intellect by a powerful conviction, but only submits to it abundant motives to win our meritorious belief; and that all those who permitted themselves to be led by the spirit of God, who yielded to divine grace, heard Him willingly and believed His words, while those who permitted themselves to be led by the spirit of Satan rejected them. Jesus, then, did not speak in parables that He might not be understood; but rather the Jews, blinded by their passions, did not wish, and did not deserve, to understand the evidence of His miracles or the meaning of His words.

Q. What is meant by the seed, and who was the sower?

A. The seed is the word of God, the teachings of the gospel, and the sower is Jesus Christ, Who once in person sowed this seed of holiness, and Who continues to sow it to the end of time by means of His ministers, who are charged with the office of His eternal priesthood.

Q. What is meant by the road, the rock, the thorns, and the good ground?

A. All these signify different kinds of Christians, who, with different dispositions, hear the divine word with greater or less or no benefit.

Q. What does the seed signify which fell by the wayside?

A. It signifies the word of God preached to those who leave their hearts open and free to vice, and are therefore always yielding to temptation. Through custom, curiosity, or accident they hear the voice of the minister of God. But the vices which rule in their hearts, like travellers who come and go, tread on and render ineffectual the great truths which are announced to them; and if these truths sometimes make impressions, the constant temptations to which hearers of this kind are subject soon obliterate them; or as the seed on the wayside is destroyed by the birds, in like manner the remembrance of the divine word received from the lips of the minister of God is plucked from their hearts by the emissaries of Satan.

Q. What of the seed that fell on the rocks?

A. This seed is the word of God heard by Christians, or rather sinners, who try to serve two masters. They hear the word of God and, touched by it, recognize their evil ways and spiritual disorders and make resolutions of amendment, but on a new occasion, at the first impulse of their favorite passions, they abandon their good resolutions and return to their former sins. The divine word would take root and grow in them if it had a foundation in charity, but as these hearers have not a solid and sincere love of God, the seed of the divine word is withered by the heat and fire of their passions.

Q. What of the seed that fell among thorns?

A. Thorns generally grow on sterile ground. This ground, if carefully cultivated, would be more or less fruitful. The seed fallen among thorns is soon suffocated by them. This takes place when the word of God is heard by a person who nourishes in his heart a mixture of good and evil. Let us say, for example, a man who is assiduous in his religious duties, not disordered by bad habits, but in matters of interest to himself vicious and avaricious; or a woman attentive to her duties, loving prayer, charitable to others, but ambitious, given to the fashions, fond of dress and show. The first lets the word of God increase in his heart as long as it does not go contrary to his interests; but finally an unjust gain, or a disregard of the rights of others, destroys every good germ. The second, on the occasion of a passion, a ball, or a too free conversation, forgets God and permits to be suffocated the seed which for a time grew in her heart. Christians of this kind, infected with thorns, are the most numerous in the world.

Q. And what of the seed that fell upon good ground?

A. By good ground, says St. Thomas, is meant the good conscience and true heart of the just man. This man, willingly, with devotion, docility, and a desire to profit by it, hears the divine word. He keeps it in his memory, meditates on it, and at the proper time recalls it in order to avoid sin, to exercise himself in virtue, and to gain merit, and in this way makes it flourish and abound.

Q. What are we to learn from this Gospel?

A. First of all, we should try to learn to which of these four classes of Christians we belong; whether to those indicated by the wayside, the rocks, the thorns, or the good ground, and when we discover our defects we should pray God to grant us the necessary grace and help to amend our lives.

Q. What should we do besides?

A. We should try to make our hearts the good ground, that the seed of the divine word may flourish and bear fruit. To do this we should be anxious to hear the word of God as frequently as possible, and to hear it not merely through custom or curiosity, but from a sincere desire to be enlightened, corrected, improved, and sanctified. For this reason we should hear the voice of the priest with humility, faith, devotion, and attention. And after having heard the divine word we should make it a duty to meditate on it, to obey it, and to render to God the fruit of good works, laboring with a good will for Him, and persevering in good to the end, that is, the harvest time.

QUINQUAGESIMA SUNDAY.

Gospel: St. Luke xviii. 31-43.

AT that time: "Jesus took unto Him the twelve and said to them: Behold we go up to Jerusalem, and all things shall be accomplished which were written by the prophets concerning the Son of man. For He shall be delivered to the Gentiles, and shall be mocked, and scourged, and spit upon. And after they have scourged Him, they will put Him to death and the third day He shall rise again. And they understood none of these things, and this word was hid from them, and they understood not the things that were said. Now it came to pass when He drew nigh to Jericho, a certain blind man sat by the wayside, begging. And when he heard the multitude passing by, he asked what this meant. And they told him that Jesus of Nazareth was passing by. And he cried out, saying: Jesus, Son of David, have mercy on me. And they that went before rebuked him, that he should hold his peace. But he cried out much more: Son of David, have mercy on me. And Jesus standing commanded him to be brought unto Him. And when he was come near, He asked him, saying: What wilt thou that I do to thee? But he said: Lord, that I may see. And Jesus said to him: Receive thy sight: thy faith hath made thee whole. And immediately he saw, and followed Him, glorifying God. And all the people, when they saw it, gave praise to God."

Q. Under what circumstances did Our Lord say these things to His apostles?

A. He said them when He was about departing from the city of Ephrem, where, after calling Lazarus back to life, and wishing to escape the envy of the Pharisees, He went for the last time to Jerusalem to suffer the full bitterness of His Passion.

Q. If He foresaw the cruel death that awaited Him there, why did He go?

A. He went there because it was the will of His Eternal Father, because this was the object of His mission on earth, and because it was the desire of His heart to sacrifice His life for the salvation of mankind.

Q. Why did He foretell to the apostles the sufferings He was to undergo in Jerusalem?

A. That they might know that He was truly the Son of God, as God alone could know future events depending on free causes. He also foretold them that the apostles might know that if He went to submit to suffering and death He did so of His own free will, and that they might not be scandalized by His humiliations, and not waver in their faith. And lastly, He foretold these things that they might learn of Him to bear courageously the sufferings and the martyrdom which they were to undergo.

Q. What are we to learn from this?

A. To strengthen ourselves always the more in

our faith by understanding that Jesus Christ is true God, and that He suffered death because He willed to do so out of love for us; and that we might learn from Him to meet courageously the tribulations and crosses which Divine Providence, always just and kind, had prepared for us.

Q. The blind man he met and cured on the way, of what was he a figure?

A. According to St. Gregory he was a figure of two things. In general, he represented the whole human race; in particular, he was a figure of those Christians who, blinded by the things of this world, do not see the value of heavenly things.

Q. How was he a figure of the whole human race?

A. Consider attentively this blind man. He was outside the city; he did not see the rags that covered him; he did not see the dangers about him; he was helpless and depended entirely on the assistance of those he met on the road. Such is the human race. Through the sin of Adam it was placed outside the way of Paradise; blinded in intellect, it sees not its own misery, nor the light of truth, nor the gulf open before it by ignorance, passion, and its own fallen nature; incapable of repairing its misfortunes by its own power, it could only hope for salvation from the Eternal Word, Who, coming upon earth clothed in our flesh, should redeem it, by His infinite merits and by the power of His grace, from its great calamity, and enable it to see God, to see itself, and to see all things necessary to salvation.

Q. How did the blind man represent those Christians who are blinded by the things of this world?

A. He saw neither the magnificence of his country, nor the road that leads to it, nor the face of any one from whom he could ask assistance. It is the same with Christians who are blinded by the things of this world. They find themselves in the bosom of the Church, but see not its beauties; they are on the road to heaven, but cannot advance one step; they wish for happiness, but know not the vanity, the impotence, the nothingness of riches, honors, and power, from which they hope for it in vain.

Q. What are we to learn from this blind man?

A. We should learn never to let a favorable opportunity pass nor delay a single moment to implore the healing of our souls whenever God passes with His grace; we should learn to make ourselves heard by prayer, internal aspirations, and by the voice of the priest.

Q. The blind man cried out with a loud voice. What is the lesson of this?

A. We should learn that when it is a question of salvation we should pay no regard to human respect nor the dissuasions of bad companions, nor to what the world may say, nor to the voice of the passions, nor to anything whatever. The greater the obstacles the greater should be our ardor to pray and invoke the divine assistance.

Q. But was not this blind man somewhat bold?

A. In appealing to Christ the Son of David He gave signs of great faith, because He thus confessed Him to be the expected Messias, capable of curing him if He so willed; and by appealing to His pity and showing his great desire he gave proof of his confidence that the Lord by His omnipotence could, and by His charity would, heal Him. We learn from this miracle to confide in the divine mercy, and know that, however great our spiritual blindness, God will give us grace if we ask it with confidence.

FIRST SUNDAY OF LENT.

Gospel: St. Matthew iv. 1-11.

AT that time: "Jesus was led by the spirit into the desert, to be tempted by the devil. And when He had fasted forty days and forty nights, afterwards He was hungry. And the tempter coming said to Him: If thou be the Son of God, command that these stones be made bread. Who answered and said: It is written: Not in bread alone doth man live, but in every word that proceedeth from the mouth of God. Then the devil took Him up into the holy city and set Him upon the pinnacle of the temple, and said to Him: If thou be the Son of God, cast Thyself down, for it is written: That He hath given His angels charge over Thee, and in their hands shall they bear Thee up, lest perhaps Thou dash Thy foot against a stone. Jesus said to him: It is written again: Thou shalt not tempt the Lord thy God. Again the devil took Him up into a very high mountain: and showed Him all the kingdoms of the world, and the glory of them, and said to Him: All these will I give Thee, if falling down Thou wilt adore me. Then Jesus saith to him: Begone, Satan, for it is written: The Lord thy God shalt thou adore, and Him only shalt thou serve. Then the devil left Him: and behold, angels came and ministered to Him."

Q. When did these events take place?

A. They took place before Jesus began His public life, and immediately after He had been baptized by

John the Baptist, when the voice of His heavenly Father was heard saying, "This is My beloved Son, in Whom I am well pleased."

Q. What spirit led Christ into the desert?

A. It was the Holy Ghost, the same Spirit Who descended upon Him in the form of a dove; it was that Holy Ghost Who inspires Christians to be faithful to the grace of baptism, to flee the world, to seek solitude, if not of the body, at least of the heart, to do penance, and to find happiness in prayer and in communion with God.

Q. But why did the Spirit lead Him into the desert where He was to be tempted?

A. The Holy Ghost Who led Christ had not His temptation in view, but His victory. The divine Redeemer had come to repair the disgrace and ignominy of the human race, and it was necessary that the evil spirit, who had overcome mankind in the person of Adam, should himself be vanquished by man in the person of Jesus Christ. It was therefore proper, says St. Gregory, that the divine Word made flesh should go to attack our enemy, and, fighting as one of us, triumph for us, and by overcoming the tempter secure to us the victory.

Q. Had Christ any other object in exposing Himself to the assaults of the enemy?

A. He had. In permitting the evil spirit to assail Him He would teach His followers not to lose courage when assailed by temptations, for as long as they do not yield to them they do not defile the soul, but are an occasion of glory and reward to brave soldiers. He also wished to teach us how to overcome the devil. He wished, as St. Augustine says, to render our victories easy for us by His own victory. He wished to teach that all who consecrate themselves to Him, and especially those who are called to do great things in the Church, should be always ready to meet temptations, for by suffering temptations they learn how to overcome them, and are able to teach others. By overcoming temptations we advance in virtue and gain greater graces and rewards.

Q. What did Christ merit for us by His long fast?

A. By His fast He sanctified our fasts, mortifications, and abstinences when we practise them in a true spirit of penance. His example renders easy for us those sufferings by which we conquer the rebellion of the flesh. Lastly, by His fast He instituted and blessed that fast of forty days which the Church has always observed as an apostolic tradition.

Q. What should we learn from Christ's first answer to the devil?

A. Satan, taking occasion of Christ's hunger, tempted Him to change stones into bread. Christ answered that man lives not by bread alone, but by every word that proceedeth from the mouth of God. This answer teaches us to put our confidence in God in all our necessities. He will provide for all our wants. How many anxieties and sins we would avoid if in our troubles we would put our confidence in God! Let us, then, live the life of the just; let us abandon ourselves without reserve to the mercy of our heavenly Father, and remember that a just man has never been forsaken by God.

Q. What are we to learn from the answer to the second temptation?

A. That we should never tempt God. Christ could

have come down from the pinnacle of the temple by the ordinary way, and it was tempting God to expect Him to work an unnecessary miracle to preserve Him if He had cast Himself down from that height, as the devil tempted Him to do. Thus also do we tempt God when we ask for miracles in confirmation of our religion, as faith is sufficient for us. We also tempt God when we ask to be cured of sickness by a miracle when we can be cured by proper medicines. We tempt God when we expect Him to preserve us from sin while we place ourselves unnecessarily in the proximate occasion of sin.

Q. What does Christ teach us by His answer to the last temptation?

A. He teaches us that we should not for all the world give to creatures the honor which belongs to God alone. The devil promised Christ all the kingdoms of the earth if falling down He would adore him, and Christ by putting him to flight taught us that we must renounce all things rather than fail to honor God. How often does the devil repeat this temptation by representing to us the temporal advantages to be gained by failing in our duty to God and by promising us the friendship and protection of the great and powerful of the world! Let us learn from Jesus that, come what may, we must never be disobedient or wanting in respect to the awful majesty of the Lord.

Q. Is there anything more to be said regarding the nature of the temptations mentioned in this Gospel?

A. We may observe that Christ, by overcoming them, has vanquished in their very foundations all the temptations that can possibly assail man. If we will but reflect we will see that temptations always arise from love of the flesh, from love of honors, or from love of the things of this world, riches. Now Christ, by refusing to change stones into bread to satisfy His hunger, overcame love of the flesh. By refusing to cast Himself down from the summit of the temple in order that the angels might bear Him up, and thus glorify Himself, He conquered love of honors. And by refusing all the kingdoms of the earth, he conquered love of worldly possessions. Thus He overcame in their very origin the principal passions that wage a continual war against us. And by the merits of His victory He has enabled us to meet by the grace of God those temptations which may come upon us.

Q. What are we to understand by those angels who came to serve Jesus?

A. By them we are to understand the way God treats those who, in the hour of temptation make good use of His grace and remain faithful to Him. He ordinarily gives peace and joy to those who have fought the good fight and resisted temptation. Joseph remained faithful when tempted, and was put into prison, but afterward the throne of Egypt was his reward. Susanna remained faithful, and suffered the agonies of death; but Daniel made her innocence known to all. The three children of Babylon remained faithful, and an angel rescued them from the fiery furnace. Let us remain faithful in the time of temptation, and the peace, happiness, and blessings we shall enjoy will be so many invisible angels which the Lord will send to comfort and console us after the battle is over.

Q. What lesson should we draw from this Gospel?

A. We should learn to love and practise mortification and penance, and not to lose courage when strongly tempted. We should repel the suggestions of the devil with the maxims and precepts of the gospel, and look to God for the reward of having suffered and endured for His glory.

SECOND SUNDAY OF LENT.

Gospel: St. Matthew xvii. 1–9.

AT that time: "Jesus taketh unto Him Peter and James, and John his brother, and bringeth them up into a high mountain apart: and He was transfigured before them. And His face did shine as the sun: and His garments became white as snow. And behold there appeared to them Moses and Elias talking with Him. And Peter answering, said to Jesus: Lord, it is good for us to be here: if Thou wilt, let us make here three tabernacles, one for Thee, and one for Moses, and one for Elias. And as He was yet speaking, behold a bright cloud overshaded them. And lo, a voice out of the cloud saying: This is My beloved Son, in Whom I am well pleased: hear ye Him. And the disciples hearing, fell upon their face, and were very much afraid. And Jesus came and touched them, and said to them: Arise, and fear not. And they, lifting up their eyes, saw no one, but only Jesus. And as they came down from the mountain Jesus charged them, saying: Tell the vision to no man till the Son of man be risen from the dead."

Q. On what mountain did this wonderful event take place?

A. It is generally believed that it took place on Mount Thabor, which is near the town of Nazareth, in the tribe of Zabulon between the Mediterranean Sea and the Lake of Genesareth. From its summit one can see almost the whole of Palestine: to the east the River Jordan and the country beyond; to the south, the tribes of Issachar and Manasses; to the west, the Mediterranean Sea; and to the north, a sweep of land reaching to the mountains of Lebanon.

Q. Why did Christ wish His transfiguration to take place on a mountain and in the presence of His three apostles?

A. He wished it to take place on a mountain, and in a solitary place, to give us to understand that divine favors are reserved for those who, by their virtues, raise themselves above all things earthly, who retire into solitude and flee from the distractions and cares of the world. Now St. Peter represents those who are steadfast in their faith, St. James those who control their passions, St. John the chaste and pure. Hence Jesus selected them to enjoy so great a privilege in order that we might hope to receive His special favors if we are firm in our faith like St. Peter, if we overcome our passions like St. James, and if we are pure in mind and body like St. John.

Q. Why did Christ manifest Himself in His glory to these apostles?

A. He did so for several reasons. First, by giving them a manifestation of the glory which was His own and which was not lost or diminished, but only hidden by the veil of humanity, He gave them a visible proof of His divinity. Moreover, He did so to strengthen them and sustain their faith when they would later on see Him in humiliation and suffering. Lastly, He was transfigured before them to encourage them and all future Christians to suffer voluntarily the trials of the apostleship and observe the law, by permitting them to see a glimpse of that consolation which they will enjoy in the vision of God, which is the reward of all that love and obey Him here on earth.

Q. What did Christ do to thus transform Himself?

A. He permitted a ray of His divinity to manifest itself from His body, and this was sufficient to cause Him to appear to the eyes of the apostles as luminous as the sun and His garments as white as snow. Imagine the effect when the sun descends beyond a mountain whose summit is capped with snow. The crest of the mountain is covered with a border of light which dazzles and charms, and you perceive that as the rays of the sun pass over the snow they impart to it their light and thus reveal colors so various and charming to see. In like manner the light of the divinity illuminated the body and garments of Jesus Christ.

Q. Why did He cause Moses and Elias to appear instead of other renowned persons?

A. Moses was the promulgator of the law which God gave him on Mount Sinai, and Elias was considered by all as the prince of the prophets. The Mosaic law prepared the way for the promised Messias, and all the sacrifices prescribed by it were but figures of the sacrifice of Jesus Christ. All the predictions of the prophets pointed to Jesus Christ. In view of these facts you can easily see that Our Lord caused Moses and Elias, and not others, to appear on either side of Him in order that the apostles, and all believers with them, could see how the figures of the law and the predictions of the prophets were to be realized in Him, and that while He was pleased to manifest His glory He called to do Him homage those who by the law and by the prophecies had prepared the way for Him.

Q. What is to be said of St. Peter, who wished to remain on the mountain enjoying that vision?

A. The magnificence of the vision, the joy of soul, and satisfaction of heart had affected him to such a degree that, forgetting that he was a man subject to death, and desiring nothing more, he thought it good to remain there forever. But if a single ray of the glory of Christ could cause such profound emotions in St. Peter, what will our joy be when at the resurrection we shall arise immortal and see Him in the fulness of His majesty, sitting on the right hand of His Father amid the splendor of the saints?

Q. What was the bright cloud?

A. Let us not lose time inquiring what it was, but rather consider what it signified. Interpreters agree that in this, as in the baptism of Christ, the Blessed Trinity manifested Itself. The Eternal Father spoke, the Divine Word was present in the person of Christ, and the Holy Ghost appeared in the semblance of a bright cloud, as He appeared in the form of a dove at the baptism of Christ. In seeing this cloud that environed Christ, Moses, Elias, the apostles, and the mountain, let us remember that Holy Spirit Who moved the lips of the prophets, Who made the law fruitful, Who crowned the great work of redemption, Who transformed the apostles, and Who animates, governs, and sanctifies the whole Church of Jesus Christ.

Q. Whose voice was it that issued from the cloud, and what was the import of the words?

A. The voice was that of the Eternal Father, for He alone could say: "This is My beloved Son in Whom I am well pleased, hear ye Him." St. Leo the Great says that by these words the Eternal Father wished to proclaim to the whole world, This is My beloved Son, not adopted, but My own, not created, but generated; this is My Son, by Whom all things were made, in Him I am well pleased, Whose words bear witness of Me, Whose humility glorifies Me. Hear ye Him because He is the Truth and the Way. He is My wisdom, He Who was foretold by the prophets and Who redeemed the world by His blood. He opens the way to heaven and by His cross gives us the means to enter into the kingdom of heaven. How unfortunate we shall be if we do not listen to this, the only Teacher of truth and of life everlasting!

Q. What is to be said of the fear which possessed the apostles?

A. It was quite natural that the apostles should have been awed by the unexpected voice of God, and we should in no way be surprised at it. We have reason, however, to be astonished that so many Christians are not frightened at hearing the menaces of the same God against those who follow not the teaching and the law of Jesus Christ.

Q. Why did Our Redeemer forbid the apostles to speak of what they had seen until after His resurrection?

A. St. Jerome says that this event was so great and wonderful that none would have believed it if the apostles had told them of it, and the ignorant especially would have been greatly scandalized at seeing Him so utterly humiliated in the time of His Passion after having manifested such great power and glory. The proper time to publish so wonderful an event was after the Resurrection, for then those who saw Him raised from the dead could have no difficulty in acknowledging Him to be the true God, and able to transfigure Himself as He did on Mount Thabor. Besides, to witness that glorious vision was a special privilege granted to the three apostles alone, and Christ forbade them to speak of it that they might learn to hide from others the special favors they had received, in order not to expose themselves to vainglory and perhaps to the envy of others. From this we should learn to conceal the secret consolations and graces which the Lord is pleased to grant us. When God grants us favors let us be thankful for them and correspond with them, but let us keep all in the inmost recesses of our hearts.

THIRD SUNDAY OF LENT.

Gospel: St. Luke xi. 14-28.

AT that time: "Jesus was casting out a devil, and the same was dumb. And when He had cast out the devil the dumb spoke: and the multitudes were in admiration at it. But some of them said: He casteth out devils by Beelzebub, the prince of devils. And others tempting asked of Him a sign from heaven. But He seeing their thoughts said to them: Every kingdom divided against itself shall be brought to desolation, and house upon a house shall fall. And if Satan also be divided against himself, how shall his kingdom stand? because you say that through Beelzebub I cast out devils.

Now if I cast out devils by Beelzebub, by whom do your children cast them out? Therefore they shall be your judges. But if I by the finger of God cast out devils, doubtless the kingdom of God is come upon you. When a strong man armed keepeth his court, those things are in peace which he possesseth. But if a stronger than he come upon him and overcome him, he will take away all his armor wherein he trusted, and will distribute his spoils. He that is not with Me is against Me; and he that gathered not with Me, scattereth. When the unclean spirit is gone out of a man he walketh through places without water, seeking rest: and not finding, he saith: I will return into my house whence I came out. And when he is come he findeth it swept and garnished. Then he goeth and taketh with him seven other spirits more wicked than himself, and entering in they dwell there. And the last state of that man becometh worse than the first. And it came to pass as He spoke these things, a certain woman from the crowd lifting up her voice said to Him: Blessed is the womb that bore Thee and the paps that gave thee suck. But He said: Yea, rather, blessed are they who hear the word of God and keep it."

Q. What is to be said of this dumb man possessed by the devil?

A. From the context of the other Gospels we learn that this unfortunate man was not only dumb but also blind, and that his condition was not the result of sickness but the work of the devil by whom he was possessed. St. Jerome, speaking of this man's recovery, says that three miracles were worked in him. The blind was made to see, the dumb to speak, and the possessed delivered from the power of the devil.

Q. Of whom is this dumb man a figure?

A. He is a figure of the human race, which, being a victim of the demon, like a blind man cannot see its own misery nor the infamy of its morals, nor the light of truth, nor its duties, nor God. And like a dumb man, it cannot utter a word in praise of the divine majesty, nor a word in behalf of its own welfare. In a more particular sense, the dumb man was a figure of those sinners who, blinded by their passions, cannot see things pertaining to God or to their own souls, and being mute in matters of religion, they open not their lips to confess their sins, to praise God, or to implore His mercy. Let us pray God that He may not permit us to become blind and dumb like so many unfortunate brethren.

Q. What are we to think of those who said that Christ healed the dumb man by the power of the devil?

A. We must not be astonished at this. They were always influenced by envy and hatred, and saw nothing but evil in the most innocent and holy actions. Let us bring the matter home to ourselves and consider how we judge our neighbors. If we find that we are inclined to interpret their actions in a good sense let us rejoice, for it is a sign that we have Christian charity in our hearts. But if we discover in us a disposition to find fault with our neighbors' actions, or to attribute bad motives to them, we may know that it is hatred and envy that inspire us, and we should pray God to free us from such inspirations.

Q. How did Christ refute their calumny?

A. By the words related in the Gospel Christ proved that it was impossible for the demon to contend against himself; that he could not be put to flight except by the power of God, and that if He, Christ, could cast out devils, then the time foretold by the prophets had come—the time when God would reign in men's hearts by His grace.

Q. Who is that strong man in armor who guards his house in peace?

A. This strong man is the devil, who had made himself master of the world by keeping almost the whole human race in bondage through errors of the mind and the power of the passions. As long as he could keep alive superstition, idolatry, and licentiousness among men he enjoyed in peace his tyrannical power over them, and they served him and plunged into the mire of corruption, without even knowing the misery and infamy of their condition, and without the desire to escape from it.

Q. And who is the stronger man who comes to take away his armor?

A. It is Jesus Christ, Who by His doctrine, example, passion, merits, and grace disarms the devil and overcomes him, destroys his kingdom, encourages us, dissipates the darkness of ignorance, banishes idolatry, and makes children of God those who before had been the slaves of sin and victims of perdition.

Q. What did Christ mean by adding: "He that is not with Me is against Me, He that gathereth not with Me scattereth"?

A. By these words He gave the Jews to understand that He did not cast out devils by the power of the devil, as they thought, for it is impossible that those can be in harmony who follow opposite ways and have opposite ends in view. In fact, says St. Jerome, the devil wants men to be the slaves of their passions, and Jesus wants them to control and overcome their passions. The devil teaches idolatry, and Jesus proclaims the knowledge of the one only true God. The devil entices men to sin, and Jesus exhorts them to practise virtue and to be just. How, then, can those agree whose purposes are so opposite?

Q. Is there, then, nothing in those words for us?

A. There is a great deal. By those words Jesus declares as enemies all those who do not think as He does and who do not agree with Him in every act. He was zealous for the glory of His Father, and in all His words, actions, and sufferings sought nothing but that glory. They, therefore, who combat His doctrines, who are indifferent in matters of religion, who work for selfish motives or to gratify their passions, are His enemies and against Him. He who does not work in the spirit of Christ, with His motives, and in His company, gains nothing, loses all, and is against Him.

Q. Who is that impure spirit who leaves a house and wanders through desert places and finds not rest?

A. It is the demon, who, driven by virtue of penance from the soul of the converted sinner, feels tormented by the desire to return and take possession again, and for this purpose redoubles His temptation, and his rabid desire to regain control of the soul leaves him no peace. Let the repentant sinner be on his guard and never cease to pray for the grace of perseverance. Let him remember that the devil knows well his weak points, and will not cease to attack him there.

Q. What means his return with seven devils worse than himself?

A. It means that when the sinner, who by God's

grace has been converted and reconciled with his Maker, falls back into sin, his last state is worse than the first; and as relapse in diseases of the body is more dangerous and more difficult to cure than the original disease, so is the relapse of the soul more fatal and difficult to heal.

Q. And the woman who cried out: "Blessed is the womb that bore thee," of whom was she a figure?

A. She was a figure of the Church, who so highly and justly praises the Blessed Virgin, who bore and nurtured the divine Redeemer, the cause of our salvation. We should enter into the spirit of the Church and bless the Mother of God, and have recourse to her with childlike confidence.

Q. And what does the answer of Jesus signify?

A. The answer implies that, though great was the happiness of the Blessed Virgin in having given birth to the Redeemer, yet the happiness of those is also very great who hear the word of God and put it in practice, for by so doing they conceive in their heart, in a spiritual manner, that Fountain and Source of all good Which the Mother of God bore in her chaste womb.

FOURTH SUNDAY OF LENT.

Gospel: St. John vi. 1-15.

AT that time: "Jesus went over the Sea of Galilee, which is that of Tiberias: and a great multitude followed Him, because they saw the miracles which He did on them that were diseased. Jesus therefore went up into a mountain, and there He sat with His disciples. Now the Pasch, the festival day of the Jews, was near at hand.

When Jesus therefore had lifted up His eyes, and seen that a very great multitude cometh to Him, He said to Philip: Whence shall we buy bread, that these may eat? And this He said to try him, for He Himself knew what He would do. Philip answered Him: Two hundred pennyworth of bread is not sufficient for them, that every one may take a little. One of His disciples, Andrew, the brother of Simon Peter, saith to Him: There is a boy here that hath five barley loaves and two fishes: but what are these among so many? Then Jesus said: Make the men sit down. Now there was much grass in the place. The men therefore sat down, in number about five thousand. And Jesus took the loaves and when He had given thanks, He distributed to them that were sat down: in like manner also of the fishes as much as they would. And when they were filled, He said to His disciples: Gather up the fragments that remain, lest they be lost. They gathered up therefore, and filled twelve baskets with the fragments of the five barley loaves, which remained over and above to them that had eaten. Now those men, when they had seen what a miracle Jesus had done, said: This is of a truth the Prophet that is to come into the world. Jesus therefore, when He knew that they would come to take Him by force and make Him king, fled again into the mountain Himself alone."

Q. What is to be said of the multitude that followed Christ into the desert?

A. We must admire their great desire to hear the words of Christ and to be with Him, a desire that caused them to undergo willingly the fatigue and inconveniences of the journey and to lay aside their worldly cares. We must deplore the negligence of so many Christians, who show no desire to follow Christ in the way of salvation and to hear His word announced by His ministers.

Q. Why did the evangelist record the circumstance that the Paschal feast or Easter was near at hand when Christ worked the miracle?

A. The multiplication of the bread in the desert, and at the time when Easter was near at hand, was a figure of the Blessed Sacrament with which the whole Christian Church would celebrate the Christian Easter, and which would feed and nourish the whole world in the desert of this life, as the multitude was fed beyond the Jordan. In feeding that multitude Christ enlivened our faith, increased our gratitude, and favored us in favoring them.

Q. Why did Christ ask Philip where they could procure bread enough to feed so great a multitude?

A. Our divine Redeemer had resolved to work a miracle, but He wished to call the attention of the apostles to the pressing want of the people and to the impossibility of providing for them by any human means, and that Philip should show repentance, for if he believed his Master to be God and Man, he should have known that it was an easy matter for Him to work a miracle to feed the multitude. Let us learn from this that God very often withholds His help that we may know our helplessness, and to convince us that when we are freed from evils of soul or body it is not the results of our own endeavors or knowledge, but of the mercy and goodness of God. Let us learn to be ready to give Him a proof of our faith whenever He is pleased to try us.

Q. Jesus gave thanks when He took the five loaves and two fishes. What are we to learn from this?

A. We should learn to do the same when we take our meals. As the people received the food from the hands of Christ, so also do we receive it from God alone in the ordinary way of His providence, for without His blessing the earth would be barren and unproductive. Jesus then thanked the Eternal Father for having placed Him in such a situation as to provide for the people by a miracle that would benefit both their souls and bodies. In the same manner must we thank God when we are able to assist the poor, and the most sincere and meritorious thanksgiving is to be prompt and generous in helping them for God's sake.

Q. Why did Christ order the fragments to be collected after the people had appeased their hunger?

A. By this our divine Master has taught us how highly we should prize all things that come from God. Besides, those fragments were an additional proof of the miracle, and are a lesson to pious people not to neglect the smallest favors of God, the inspirations and fervor in prayer, the grace of receiving the sacraments, for from the effects we will better learn the importance of the helps we have received.

Q. What does the miraculous multiplication of bread signify, when twelve basketfuls remained after all had eaten?

A. Christ has promised the charitable that their alms will be abundantly rewarded, and this fact of the Gospel is a proof of it. He distributed five loaves; each ate and was satisfied, and still there remained twelve basketfuls at His disposal. In the same manner, if we help our neighbor the the love of God our alms will relieve his wants, the act will be to our advantage, and before God we will gain a hundred-fold.

Q. Did the multitude want to make Him king because He fed them?

A. The Gospel tells us that the people, on witnessing the great miracle, thought of making Him their king, and this is precisely what Christ wants us to do. We have said that this miracle was a figure of the Blessed Sacrament. Now, when we have approached the Eucharistic table, when we have been fed with the body and blood of Christ, it is our duty to proclaim Him the King and Master and Lord of our affections, of our heart, and of our whole self.

Q. Why, then, did Jesus retire into the mountain?

A. He fled into the mountain because He came not to seek human praise or earthly honor. Let us learn from this to do all the good we can in this life, but not to seek for reward on earth—rather to flee from the applause and honor of the world, because it may make us proud and vain, and expose us to the persecutions of the jealous and envious, whose number is great.

FIFTH SUNDAY OF LENT, OR PASSION SUNDAY.

Gospel: St. John viii. 46–59.

AT that time, Jesus said to the multitude of the Jews: "Which of you shall convince Me of sin? If I say the truth to you, why do you not believe Me? He that is of God heareth the words of God. Therefore you hear them not, because you are not of God. The Jews therefore answered and said to Him: Do not we say well that Thou art a Samaritan, and hast a devil? Jesus answered: I have not a devil; but I honor My Father, and you have dishonored Me. But I seek not My own glory; there is One that seeketh and judgeth. Amen, amen, I say to you: if any man keep My word, he shall not see death forever. The Jews therefore said: Now we know that Thou hast a devil. Abraham is dead, and the prophets: and Thou sayest: If any man keep My word, he shall not taste death forever. Art Thou greater than our father Abraham, who is dead? And the prophets are dead. Whom dost Thou make Thyself? Jesus answered: If I glorify Myself, My glory is nothing. It is My Father that glorifieth Me, of Whom you say that He is your God, and you have not known Him: but I know Him; and if I shall say that I know Him not I shall be like to you, a liar. But I do know Him, and do keep His word. Abraham your father rejoiced that he might see My day: he saw it, and was glad. The Jews therefore said to Him: Thou art not yet fifty years old, and hast Thou seen Abraham? Jesus said to them: Amen, amen, I say to you, before Abraham was made, I am. They took up stones therefore to cast at Him: but Jesus hid Himself, and went out of the temple."

Q. Why did Jesus affirm His innocence and defy any one to convict Him of sin?

A. He did it to convince the Jews of their injustice in refusing to believe His words and His doctrine. When a teacher combines profound learning with a spotless life he has a right to the confidence of those who hear Him, for as a learned man there is no probability of his being deceived, and as an honest man no one should suspect that he would deceive. Let us also learn to live up to our teaching, our advice, and our corrections; so that when we reproach others, they cannot reproach us with inconsistency.

Q. Was it for this reason that He added: "Why do you not believe Me"?

A. Certainly it was. Up to that time Christ had given proof that His teaching was full of truth and heavenly wisdom, and the Gospel says that His enemies were so convinced and overpowered by His proofs that they had no longer the courage to question Him. On the other hand, His life had always been so holy, prudent, affable, and irreproachable, that no one could accuse Him of the slightest transgression of the law, or of sin. As He had shown His wisdom and His holiness of life, He had a right to be heard; and if the Jews did not believe Him, He could justly reproach them for their injustice. How many Christians deserve such a reproach from Christ!

Q. What is to be said of the sentence Christ pronounced against the Jews?

A. The sentence which declared the Jews to be strangers to God was most just, and as such it should inspire us with fear. The Jews did not believe in Christ because they were not guided by the Spirit of God, but rather by their pride, envy, and hatred; but what shall we say of ourselves if we have no inclination, no wish, to hear the word of God? What shall we say if we hear not or care not for what God teaches us by the voice of His priests, by His inspirations, etc.? We must, then, acknowledge that we are not guided by the Holy Ghost, that we do not belong to God, but rather to the devil, like the obstinate Jews. May the Lord preserve us from so great an evil!

Q. What did the Jews do when they heard that terrible sentence?

A. Instead of endeavoring to be enlightened and converted, they became still more obstinate in their impiety. Prompted by an intense hatred, they insulted the divine Redeemer by calling Him a Samaritan and one possessed by a devil. How many Christians are like the Jews! Instead of profiting by the counsel of their confessors, by the sermons and instructions of the priests, they sacrilegiously insult God, and call fanatics and impostors the ministers of the Word, the heralds of His infinite mercy or of His terrible justice.

Q. What is to be said of Christ's action in this case?

A. Insulted and calumniated as a schismatic, an apostate, and one possessed by a devil, He could, like Elias, have called fire from heaven to destroy His enemies, but He preferred to give us an example of divine patience and meekness, and refrained from saying any more to them than what the glory of God required. The charity of Jesus toward His enemies was seen on this occasion in all its greatness, and it teaches us how we should act when assailed by calumny and abuse.

Q. What is to be said of His answer?

A. Jesus was calumniated as being a Samaritan and possessed by a devil. To the first accusation He made no reply, because all knew that it was false, and because, as St. Gregory says, "As the word Samaritan signifies not only a schismatic, but also a guardian," in this latter sense, as the guardian of our souls, He did not resent this name, although apparently an opprobrious one. By so doing He taught us not to reply to imputations that are evidently false and unjust. He replied, however, to the other accusation, because had He been silent it would have been prejudicial to the mission He had received from His Father. In fact, how could He have preached the truth, how could He be the Redeemer of the world and the mediator between God and man, if He were possessed by a devil? How could the future Christians believe in Him if they knew He was so possessed? The interests of religion, therefore, required this calumny to be refuted, and on this account He did refute it, but with a meekness which one possessed by a devil could not have done. Let us learn from our divine Master to suffer false accusations for God's sake as long as they are not injurious to our character or to the interests of religion; but when silence is detrimental to truth, religion, or our neighbor, we should speak out and refute the false accusations, but always with the meekness of Jesus Christ.

Q. Why, then, did not the Jews yield when He assured them with an oath that "if any man keeps My word he shall not taste death forever"?

A. They were so carnal-minded, says St. Gregory, that they did not understand Him. Christ intended to say that whoever would faithfully observe His holy law would preserve the life of his soul—his soul would not die—but the Jews thought He spoke of the death of the body, and that He promised His followers that they would never suffer such a death. Taking His word in this sense, the blind Jews fancied that He would have them believe what was very strange and utterly impossible, as Abraham himself had to die.

Q. What did Christ mean to say by these words: "Abraham rejoiced that he might see My day, he saw it and was glad"?

A. Abraham expected the Saviour, and God assured him that the Saviour would come, nay, that He would be born of one of his descendants. Abraham lived in this faith, and in this faith he died, because, relying upon God's word, he saw with certainty in the far future that Christ by whom he was to be saved. If Abraham rejoiced thinking of the expected Messias, how can we remain indifferent when we think of the Saviour Who has come and Who has made us members of His body?

Q. But did the Jews understand these words?

A. Men who are ruled by their passions cannot understand the truth; hence the Jews, who were full of envy and hatred, did not understand these words: they thought they were strange and unpardonable. They understood Him to say that he, as man, lived in the time of Abraham and was seen by Abraham. As two thousand years had elapsed since Abraham's death, they thought this very strange. They did not think of that vision which is proper to faith. Thus one errs who relies too much upon himself and beholds things in a light different from that of a Christian.

Q. Is there not an inexactness in this phrase, "Before Abraham was made, I am"?

A. No, there is not. The phrase is perfectly correct. By these words Christ intended to make known to us that He was God, one with the Father and the Holy Ghost; that as God He was eternal and stood in need of nothing, and as eternity is as one day and admits of no time, He could truly say, "Before Abraham was made, I am." St. Augustine says: "Know the Creator, and make a distinction beween Him and the creature. He Who spoke, that is, Christ, according to His humanity was a descendant of Abraham, and as God He is eternal and existed before Abraham."

Q. What are we to think of the Jews, who upon hearing these words took up stones to cast at Him?

A. We need not be surprised at this. When a person is obstinate in his errors and hardened in sin, he ends by waging war against Christ, and attempts even, if it were possible, to destroy Him. How many, who are the slaves of their passions and wish not to amend their lives, end by denying the truth and fiercely attacking the gospel? One abyss leads to another, and he who has not the courage to overcome himself will by degrees lose his faith, hate religion, and not blush to be publicly known as an enemy of God.

Q. What is to be learned from Christ's hiding Himself and going out of the temple?

A. Who does not know that the Divine Master, Who had worked so many miracles, could in a moment have felled the impious Jews to the ground, as He afterward did the crowd in the Garden of Gethsemani, or could He not have treated them worse? Yet He preferred to hide Himself, and by so doing He taught us to be meek and not to resist the powers, even when we are sure of victory, in order not to still more irritate them and to cause them to do us greater harm when opportunity offers, which they surely will not let escape them.

PALM SUNDAY.

Gospel: St. Matthew xxi. 1–9.

AT that time: "When they drew nigh to Jerusalem, and were come to Bethphage, unto Mount Olivet, then Jesus sent two disciples, saying to them: Go ye into the village that is over against you, and immediately you shall find an ass tied, and a colt with her, loose them, and bring them to Me, and if any man shall say anything to you, say ye that the Lord hath need of them; and forthwith he will let them go. Now all this was done that it might be fulfilled which was spoken by the prophet, saying: Tell ye the daughter of Sion: Behold thy King cometh to thee, meek, and sitting upon an ass and a colt the foal of her that is used to the yoke. And the disciples, going, did as Jesus commanded them. And they brought the ass and the colt: and laid their garments upon them, and made Him sit thereon. And a very great multitude spread their garments in the way; and others cut boughs from the trees, and strewed them in the way: and the multitudes that went before, and that followed, cried, saying: Hosanna to the Son of David: blessed is He that cometh in the name of the Lord: Hosanna in the highest."

Q. What place was this Bethphage?

A. It was a village not far from Bethany, the residence of Lazarus. It was located on the side of Mount Olivet, at the head of the famous valley of Josaphat, which from there extends to the Dead Sea. In this village were kept the sheep, goats, oxen, and all the animals that were sacrificed in the temple according to the law. From this place they were solemnly led to Jerusalem, entering by the Golden Gate.

Q. Is there anything to remark on this point?

A. It was from this village that Our Saviour went to Jerusalem to be crucified the following week, and as He was the Lamb that was to be slaughtered for the salvation of the world, the victim of which all the other sacrifices of the law of Moses were only the figure, He therefore wanted to go to that place, walk on the same road, and enter the same gate which was entered by the victims destined for the sacrifice, and on that solemn day of the Paschal lamb.

Q. What do the two beasts of burden signify which Christ ordered His disciples to bring?

A. The old one, accustomed to work and carry burdens, was a figure of the Jewish nation brought up under the yoke of the Old Law and accustomed to carry the burden of its observances. The colt that was tied was a figure of the Gentiles, who up to that time had lived according to their will and known no restraint. Christ sent His disciples to bring both animals, as the apostles by preaching His resurrection and gospel would convert both the Jews and the Gentiles and unite them in His Church and make them the instruments of His glorious triumph.

Q. Had Christ any other reason to use those two animals in entering Jerusalem?

A. He intended that the prophecy of Zachary should be fulfilled. This prophet long before had said: "Rejoice greatly, O daughter of Sion! Shout for joy, O daughter of Jerusalem! Behold, thy King will come to thee, the Just and Saviour. He is poor and riding upon an ass, and upon a colt, the foal of an ass." (Zach. ix. 9.)

Q. What is to be said on these points?

A. In all this we recognize an undeniable proof of the divinity of Christ, and of His power and absolute dominion over all things. God alone sees, because present to Him, events at a distance and in the future, even those depending on free agencies. And as Christ told the apostles with certainty what they would find in the place to which He sent them, He gave a proof that He could see when He was not personally present, and that consequently He was God, as He declared. In regard to the answer His apostles should give the owner of the animals, He gave them to understand that, as God, *He* was the owner of them, and that the possessor should acknowledge having received them from Him and should give them up to Him when He required them. We should learn from this that what we possess is not really ours but God's, from Whom we received it, and that we are obliged to render it up to Him when He reclaims it.

Q. How did there happen to be so great a multitude in Jerusalem, and why did they do Christ such great honor?

A. Remember that on that same day on which Christ entered Jerusalem the Paschal lamb was led with great solemnity from Bethphage to the temple. It is not surprising, then, that our divine Saviour should meet on the same road so many people. Besides, all Jerusalem was in excitement and wonder because of the great miracle Jesus had but recently worked—the raising of Lazarus from the dead after he had been four days in the grave. The people, who revered Him on account of His other miracles, were carried to the highest pitch of admiration by this manifestation of His power over death. This triumph of the God-man had been foretold, and the omnipotent Hand that disposes of all things procured its fulfilment.

Q. What was the intention of the multitude in strewing branches of palm and olive, and spreading their garments on the road?

A. Naturally speaking, we may say that the people, wishing to pay homage to Christ and to make His entry into Jerusalem as solemn as possible, knew no other way of manifesting the feelings of their hearts. But we must raise our minds higher, and see the hand of God in things which appear so natural and accidental. Jesus went to Jerusalem to be crucified, and by His death to conquer hell, to bring down upon men the fulness of grace, and detach their hearts from the things of this world in order to direct them to heavenly things. Hence God so willed it that the great multitude should applaud the triumph of the Redeemer, and—as the Church says on this day—with palms in their hands they proclaimed His victory over Satan. The olive branches signified the oil of grace which would be diffused over the children of redemption. The garments spread under His feet signified the renunciation of all earthly affections which the just must make for God's sake; for, according to St. Gregory, earthly affections are the garments that entangle our souls, and the better to fight our spiritual enemies we must get rid of them.

Q. What are we to learn from this Gospel?

A. We must learn not to trust the world, to fear its inconstancy, and to hope for reward from God alone.

To-day we behold Christ entering Jerusalem amidst the hosannas of the people—five days later we shall see Him dragged to Mount Calvary amidst curses and blasphemies. To-day the people are all love for Him and pay Him homage—in a few days we shall see them filled with hatred, demanding His blood. To-day Christ crosses the valley of Josaphat in an humble manner, riding on a beast of burden—a day will come when, sitting upon the clouds and surrounded with glory, He will in that same valley judge the living and the dead.

Let us, therefore, learn not to trust the world, which quickly abandons what it once loved, and not to trust ourselves, who are liable to change at any moment. Let us hope from God the reward for the humiliations we have suffered upon earth.

EASTER SUNDAY.

Gospel: St. Mark xvi. 1–7.

AT that time: "Mary Magdalen, and Mary the mother of James, and Salome, bought sweet spices, that coming they might anoint Jesus. And very early in the morning, the first day of the week, they came to the sepulchre, the sun being now risen. And they said one to another: Who shall roll us back the stone from the door of the sepulchre? And looking, they saw the stone rolled back. For it was very great. And entering into the sepulchre, they saw a young man sitting on the right side, clothed with a white robe: and they were astonished. Who saith to them: Be not affrighted: you seek Jesus of Nazareth, Who was crucified. He is risen, He is not here; behold the place where they laid Him. But go, tell His disciples and Peter that He goeth before you into Galilee: there you shall see Him, as He told you."

Q. What are we to think of those women who, all alone and without fear, went at that hour to the sepulchre?

A. It shows with what truth a holy Father said: "Perfect charity knows no fear." Those holy women sincerely loved Jesus, and, wishing in some manner to show their fidelity toward Him, they went to anoint with sweet spices His inanimate body. We ought to learn from these pious women to be courageous in working for the glory of Jesus Christ, and, as St. Gregory says, "we shall bring Him precious balm if we serve Him with humility and with mortification."

Q. What is to be said of these words: "They came very early in the morning, the first day in the week, the sun being now risen"?

A. In regard to the early hour they left their homes, we should admire their true devotion, which admitted of no delay in executing their good purpose. He who sincerely serves God will never lose time; he abhors every delay that hinders him in doing all he can for God. In regard to the day, which was the first day of the week, we are to recognize that day of the Lord which afterward was to be the holy day of the Christian Church, on which we also should devote ourselves to works of religion, and bring balm to Jesus Christ. Finally, in the fact that the sun had risen, we see that a soul that sincerely seeks the glory of God will never remain in darkness, ignorance, or doubt, but will always find the light that comforts and guides it in all its steps. If, according to the laws of nature, the sun had risen, it had also risen according to the laws of grace, because Christ had already risen from the dead, and by His resurrection bestowed the full light of the gospel, confirmed the true faith, and brought the day of life to the whole world.

Q. Why did those women, on their way to the sepulchre, think only of the stone with which the tomb was closed, and not of the soldiers who guarded the tomb?

A. These women did not know that soldiers were there, or that the tomb was sealed. On Friday evening they had seen Joseph Nicodemus and other friends of Christ close the sepulchre with a large stone, but they did not know that on the following day, that is, on the Sabbath, the leaders of the Pharisees, who did not scruple to violate the sacredness of the day, had sealed the stone and placed guards at the tomb to prevent the apostles from stealing the body. Hence the pious women thought only of the difficulty of removing the large stone, and not of one still greater—the soldiers who guarded the sepulchre and would prevent their approaching. How often do we also fear imaginary difficulties, and think not of the real ones that would prevent us from doing good if God did not remove them. Let us learn from this to pray to God to remove with His powerful hand not only the obstacles which we know of, but also those which we know not of.

Q. How can we say that these women did not know that the tomb was sealed?

A. Though the Gospel says nothing of this, it is natural to suppose that they did not know it. For, if they had known, they would not conspire to break the seals, on account of their respect for public authority; besides, they would know it was impossible, on account of the opposition of the guards; and out of respect for themselves they would neither have desired nor hoped for any favor from the soldiers. The true lover of God is always respectful, intelligent, and prudent, and had these pious women conspired to break the seals, they would have offended against the public authority, which the Divine Teacher had always respected. They would have acted blindly in not calculating on resistance, and they would have been imprudent to expect favors from idolatrous soldiers who were no respecters of virtue. In addition to this they could not have thought that those Pharisees, who found fault with Christ for working miracles on the Sabbath, would themselves desecrate the sanctity of the Sabbath by sealing the tomb. And lastly, if they had faith, they should rather guard than destroy the seals which Christ, in order to increase His glory, would Himself break by rising from the tomb, as He had so often foretold. From all this we must conclude that the pious women did not know that the sepulchre had been sealed.

Q. But if they knew the difficulty of removing the stone, why did they continue their journey?

A. Behold the work of love! They knew the difficulty, but they hoped to overcome it with the divine help. One who truly loves God hopes all from God, and his hopes are never disappointed. The women came to the sepulchre and found that the heavy stone had been removed. Let us also learn to advance steadily on the way of virtue, and the obstacles which at a distance discourage us will disappear as we approach them.

Q. What does the Evangelist intend by telling us that the women entered into the sepulchre?

A. In order to understand these words we must first know how the sepulchre was made in which the body of Christ was placed. There was, not far from Mount Calvary, a place where Joseph of Arimathea had, according to the Venerable Bede, prepared a tomb for himself; he had cut into the side of a rock and cleared a space the size of a small room, or rather he cut out a round arch, in which a man standing could touch the roof with his fingers. The opening of this cave was rather small, and on the east side; upon entering, there was on the right side, that is, toward the north, a bed of marble seven feet long and three hands high, with an elevation at both ends. Upon this bed of stone, on which no one had as yet been placed, the body of Christ was laid, and, according to the custom of the Jews, the whole body, except the head, was wrapped in fine linen, with the spices brought by Nicodemus; the head was covered with a sheet that was fastened behind the shoulders and on the breast. Now imagine we see those women, who, having arrived at the sepulchre, and finding the stone removed, one by one entered the cave, and on one side saw the winding-sheets, and on the marble bed they saw a young man full of glory; and then you will understand what the Evangelist intended by saying they entered into the sepulchre.

Q. Who was that young man whom the women saw in the sepulchre?

A. He was an angel, whose countenance, as St. Matthew relates, was as lightning, and his garments as white as snow. He was seated on the right hand to indicate that the Divine Redeemer had completed His earthly career, and had received the glory which His Eternal Father had prepared for Him. His countenance was like lightning, because it was terrible to the enemies of Christ; his garments were white as snow, on account of his heavenly purity. He told the women not to fear, because he never need fear who goes in search of Christ, and only those must tremble who wage war against Him by their scandalous manner of living.

Q. What is to be said about the command the angel gave to the women?

A. The angel told the women that they should immediately give notice to the disciples, and to Peter. Here we should notice, first, the haste which the angel commanded; secondly, the person whose name is mentioned in preference to others. It was quite natural that these pious women should loiter to gaze on the empty bed of stone upon which the body of Christ had reposed, the winding-sheets in which His sacred body had been wrapped, and the cloth that had covered His most adorable head. But the angel commanded them not to lose time, and to go immediately and proclaim the resurrection of Christ. Let us learn from this that when God is pleased to send us joy and consolation we must not seek in them our own satisfaction and pleasure, but should rather give glory to God by praising His infinite mercy and love, and by acknowledging our own unworthiness. In regard to the second point, of all the apostles only Peter's name was mentioned. In this we see a proof of his primacy, and also a strong reason for him to rejoice in his deep sorrow. Was not Peter the prince of the apostles, the foundation of the new-born Church? Therefore to him should be given the joyful news which established the faith on a firm foundation. Was not Peter transfixed with sorrow on account of his sin? Therefore to him as a penitent the heavenly messenger should send the joyful tidings of Christ's resurrection. Let us learn from this angel to respect our superiors, and to have compassion for the afflicted.

Q. Did the women do promptly what they were told to do?

A. They went immediately to do the angel's bidding, but, as St. Matthew relates, on their way they met Jesus Himself, Who said to them: "All hail! Fear not, but go tell My brethren that they go into Galilee; there they will see Me."

Q. Were the pious women the first to see Christ?

A. They were. God makes no distinction of sex, age, or state of life. He who first goes in search of Christ with the fervor of charity, with devotion and the balm of holy virtue, will be the first to receive His special favors.

Q. Why did Christ on this occasion call His disciples His brethren?

A. With the exception of St. John, the conduct of the apostles during His passion was such that Christ had reason to be displeased with them; but in His great charity He had compassion on their weakness, and still loved them; and, in order to console and encourage them, He sends His greeting to them, and calls them by the endearing name *brethren*. Besides, by the death of Christ all Christians are the adopted children of the Eternal Father, and brethren of Jesus

Christ. After so great an event, this was the first time that a human eye had seen Him; hence for the first time He greets us all by that endearing name, giving us thereby to understand that by the merits of His death we have acquired a new standing, merited a new name, and have become His brethren. O God! we are but worms of the earth, but by Thy mercy we are the brethren of Jesus Christ.

FIRST SUNDAY AFTER EASTER.

Gospel: St. John xx. 19–31.

AT that time: "When it was late that same day, the first of the week, and the doors were shut where the disciples were gathered together for fear of the Jews, Jesus came and stood in the midst, and said to them: Peace be to you. And when He had said this He showed them His hands and His side. The disciples therefore were glad when they saw the Lord. He said therefore to them again: Peace be to you. As the Father hath sent Me, I also send you. When He had said this He breathed on them; and He said to them: Receive ye the Holy Ghost. Whose sins you shall forgive, they are forgiven them: and whose sins you shall retain, they are retained. Now Thomas, one of the twelve, who is called Didymus, was not with them when Jesus came. The other disciples therefore said to him: We have seen the Lord. But he said to them: Except I shall see in His hands the print of the nails, and put my finger into the place of the nails, and put my hand into His side, I will not believe. And after eight days again His disciples were within, and Thomas with them. Jesus cometh, the doors being shut, and stood in the midst, and said: Peace be to you. Then

He saith to Thomas: Put in thy finger hither, and see My hands; and bring hither thy hand and put it into My side: and be not faithless but believing. Thomas answered, and said to Him: My Lord and my God. Jesus saith to him: Because thou hast seen Me, Thomas, thou hast believed: blessed are they that have not seen and have believed. Many other signs also did Jesus in the sight of His disciples which are not written in this book. But these are written that you may believe that Jesus is the Christ the Son of God; and that believing you may have life in His name."

Q. If the doors of the room were closed, how did Christ enter?

A. We must know, says St. Augustine, that God can do many things which we cannot understand. As Jesus while yet mortal could walk on the water without sinking, and as He was able without being seen or touched to pass among those who wished to cast Him from the precipice and to stone Him in the temple, so after His glorious resurrection He could pass through closed doors and enter the room without difficulty. All is explained by the power of Christ, true God and true man.

Q. What are we to infer from the fact of the doors being closed?

A. As our senses are the doors of the soul, we infer that when these senses are closed to things of the world Jesus will enter into our souls and say: "Peace be to you." Let us, then, close our eyes in order not to see the vanities of the world, our ears not to hear them spoken of, and our lips in order not to speak useless and evil words, and Jesus will come into our hearts and announce peace to us.

Q. What are we to think of these words of Christ: "Peace be to you"?

A. By these sweet words Jesus announced the ineffable fruit of His passion, which was peace between God and ourselves. He exhorts the apostles not to be disturbed by the malice of men, and invites them to confide in Him, and not to think that He is displeased with them on account of their weakness and unfaithfulness shown during His passion. Let us beseech God that we also may experience the effect of these words, and enjoy peace with Him, with our neighbors, and with ourselves.

Q. Why did Christ after His resurrection retain the wounds in His hands, feet, and side?

A. Those wounds did not disfigure the glorious members of His body, but rather increased their beauty, and He retained them in order to show that it was by suffering that He purchased His present glory, to confirm the truth of His passion and of His resurrection, to excite continually our gratitude, and to incessantly present to the eyes of His Eternal Father the price of our souls.

Q. How are we to understand these words: "As the Father hath sent Me, I also send you"?

A. These words prove the legitimate authority of the apostles, the scope of their mission, and the manner and love with which they should accomplish it. As Christ was sent on earth by the Eternal Father, absolute Master of all things, so, in like manner, the apostles were sent by Christ, in Whose hand is placed all power on earth and in heaven. Christ taught the world by His doctrines, His miracles, and His example, and the apostles were to do and have done in like manner. Lastly, Christ completed His mission on earth by a continual prodigy of love, and the apostles and their successors should always be guided by a similar love in all their actions.

Q. Why did Christ on this occasion impart the Holy Ghost to the apostles?

A. Notice that when Christ had said, "Receive ye the Holy Ghost," He immediately added: "Whose sins you shall forgive, they are forgiven." He therefore imparted the Holy Ghost to the apostles in order to enable them to exercise with effect the judging of consciences. They were in the name of God to retain or to forgive sins, and Christ endowed them with His own spirit for so exalted a ministry; they were to communicate this same Holy Ghost to all their successors, that is, to the Bishops and Priests, in order that the authority received from Him should be exercised till the end of the world.

Q. What are we to think of the incredulity of Thomas?

A. He unfortunately sinned. He should have believed that Christ was not wanting in the power to fulfil the promises made regarding His resurrection. He should have believed the testimony of the apostles, and had less confidence in himself and more in his Divine Master. His incredulity, however, has assisted powerfully the Church, because it shows that the apostles were not hasty in believing the resurrection of the Master, but that they believed that wonderful event by the force of evidence.

Q. What signifies the eighth day, on which Christ wished Thomas to put his finger into His wounds?

A. This eighth day signifies that great day when in

heaven we shall see with our own eyes and touch with our own hands the sacred fountains of our salvation. Hence, in order to obtain so great a happiness, let us now promptly and sincerely believe all that the legitimate ministers of Christ teach us relating to life eternal. Let us not be so presumptuous as to constitute ourselves the judges in matters of faith, and let us remember that the Divine Redeemer called those blessed who have not seen and have believed.

Q. And how may we also rejoice in that peace announced to the apostles?

A. We also can enjoy that peace if, with the grace of God obtained through Christ, we study to keep in peace with God, by avoiding sin; in peace with our neighbor, by loving him with true charity and suffering with patience his defects; and in peace with ourselves, by being contented with our condition in life, and limiting the desires of our heart.

SECOND SUNDAY AFTER EASTER.

Gospel: St. John x. 11–16.

AT that time, Jesus said to the Pharisees: "I am the Good Shepherd. The good shepherd giveth his life for his sheep. But the hireling and he that is not the shepherd, whose own the sheep are not, seeth the wolf coming, and leaveth the sheep and flieth: and the wolf catcheth and scattereth the sheep. And the hireling flieth, because he is a hireling, and he hath no care for the sheep. I am the Good Shepherd: and I know Mine, and Mine know Me. As the Father knoweth Me, and I know the Father: and I lay down My life for My sheep. And other sheep I have, that are not of this fold: them also I must bring, and they shall hear My voice, and there shall be one fold and one shepherd."

Q. Why did Christ call Himself the Good Shepherd?

A. God had said by the mouth of Ezechiel: "I will set up one shepherd over them, and he shall feed them, even My servant David: he shall feed them, and he shall be their shepherd" (xxxiv. 23). According to an eloquent commentator the above words mean: "I will set up one shepherd. . . . David will be this shepherd, not David who is dead, but that David Who was expected from the beginning of the world, and Whom all the prophets have foretold; He Who in the Holy Scriptures is often called by the name of His royal ancestor. I speak of the Redeemer of mankind, of the Redeemer of the world, of Him Who gathers all My sheep into the great fold of the Church, whose boundaries are the confines of the earth. . . . My son, born of My own substance, equal to Me in all things, Who assumed the form of a servant from the blood of David, He will come to feed My new people, to govern them, to defend them, and to be a faithful and loving shepherd to them." Hence, when Christ said, "I am the Good Shepherd," His intention was to formally announce to His hearers, and at the same time to the whole world, that He was the Shepherd promised by the Eternal Father, that is, the only-begotten Son of God, Who, becoming man, and Who as man was of the house of David, would teach the whole world, and gather all nations into the one fold of His Church. Hence the Jews were guilty in not recognizing Him. In vain do they even now expect Him; and we are the fortunate ones who by the grace of God acknowledge Jesus

Christ to be the only Shepherd Who was promised and announced in all the prophecies.

Q. Why does Christ say that the good shepherd gives his life for his sheep?

A. Here Christ describes a good shepherd in order to make it known that He must be acknowledged as such. The good shepherd who cares for his sheep leads them to good pastures, he leads them to the water to quench their thirst, and to defend them from the wolf he will expose his own life; for at beholding the wolf he flies to the spot armed with his staff and followed by his dogs, and gives battle to the ferocious brute at the risk of his own life. Now Jesus has done the same for us, only in a more sublime manner. He loved us with so great a love as to assume the form of a servant; He led us on the way of virtue by His own example; He feeds us with His holy doctrine, with His grace, and with His own flesh; He quenches our thirst at the fountains of the holy sacraments, and to save us from the infernal dragon He took up His cross, went to encounter the enemy, sacrificed His own life, and by His ministers He continually protects us from the attacks of him who threatens us with death.

Q. Why did Christ describe the hireling?

A. By so doing He in the first place proves that He is the Good Shepherd, because the qualities of the hireling cannot be applied to Him, inasmuch as He has shown that His conduct was quite different from that of a man who does his work for gain, pride, and self-love. In the second place, He has taught His ministers what they should be to the sheep under their care, and how, by examining the motive of their actions, and the manner in which they perform them, they can judge whether they are good shepherds, zealous for the welfare of souls, or whether they are hirelings who in all things seek themselves.

Q. Why does Christ say that He knows His sheep and that they know Him?

A. A good shepherd knows each of his sheep in particular, and calls it by name. Hence he knows which are the best, the indifferent, and the poorest, he knows which are the strong, the fruitful, and the defective, and when one goes astray he immediately knows it and goes in search of it. He provides for the weak, and carries on his shoulders the sick. Christ is all this in regard to us, His fortunate sheep. He knows each individual soul, its qualities, its merits, its defects, and its wants. If it goes astray He mercifully seeks it; if it is weak He assists it Himself, and helps it by His ministers; if it is sick He treats it with His holy sacraments. In a word, He lovingly provides for all its wants.

Q. What is to be said of the sheep that know Him?

A. The sheep know their shepherd by his countenance, his voice, and his call; hence if they hear him they obey, they remain where they are, or they come to him, according as he may order; if the wolf comes they run to the shepherd for protection, and he places himself at their head and sets the dogs on the aggressor. Lastly, the sheep, who fear all else, have no fear of their shepherd; they permit him to take them, to shear and handle them as he pleases. In the same manner do the true Christians know Jesus Christ by His virtues, His commands, His voice, and even by His chastisements. Whether favored, called, or chastised, they know whence all comes. Let us always look up to Christ, let us confide in Him, have recourse to Him, and patiently receive from His hand all that afflicts us.

Q. What did Jesus mean when He said: "As the Father knoweth Me, and I know the Father: and I lay down My life for My sheep"?

A. According to St. Cyril, Christ intended to say that as the Father knows Him to be His Son, consubstantial with Himself, and the first-born of the elect, in the same manner does He know God as His Father Who loves Him, and by loving Him loves all His adopted children, and that in the same manner does He know His sheep as His members and the object of His love, and His sheep know Him to be their Shepherd, their Head and the Source of their life. On account of this knowledge He laid down His life for His sheep, and they know that it was sacrificed for their welfare. Would to God that we had a lively knowledge of this! Our gratitude would be more sincere and efficacious, and our lives more holy.

Q. Of whom did Jesus speak when He said that He had other sheep that He would bring into the fold?

A. He spoke of the Gentiles who did not then belong to His flock, but who through the apostles would hear His voice, know the truth, embrace the faith, and by baptism enter the Church, so that the Jews and Gentiles would form but one people and He would be the loving Father of all, and thus there would be only one fold and one shepherd.

Q. What are we to learn from all this?

A. First, what a great happiness it is to belong to a shepherd so loving, powerful, and solicitous for our salvation. Secondly, we should constantly thank our good God for His great mercy. Lastly, we should show ourselves loving and obedient sheep. And as the sheep repay the shepherd for his care and labor in their behalf, so should we, by our affections, good works, and resignation to the dispositions of Divine Providence, repay in a manner the sacrifices which Christ underwent for us.

THIRD SUNDAY AFTER EASTER.

Gospel: St. John xvi. 16–22.

AT that time, Jesus said to His disciples: "A little while, and you shall not see Me; and again a little while, and you shall see Me: because I go to the Father. Then some of His disciples said one to another: What is this that He saith to us: A little while, and you shall not see Me: and again a little while, and you shall see Me, and, because I go to the Father? They said therefore: What is this that He saith, A little while? We know not what He speaketh. And Jesus knew that they had a mind to ask Him, and He said to them: Of this do you inquire among yourselves, because I said: A little while, and you shall not see Me; and again a little while, and you shall see Me? Amen, amen, I say to you, that you shall lament and weep, but the world shall rejoice; and you shall be made sorrowful, but your sorrow shall be turned into joy. A woman, when she is in labor, hath sorrow, because her hour is come: but when she hath brought forth the child, she remembereth no more the anguish, for joy that a man is born into the world. So also you now indeed have sorrow, but I will see you again, and your heart shall rejoice: and your joy no man shall take from you."

Q. When and why did Jesus say this to the apostles?

A. Our Saviour said these words to the apostles a few hours before His passion, that is, shortly after the Last Supper and before He left the supper room to go to the Garden of Gethsemani. He spoke to them in this manner to console them for the sufferings they were to endure during His passion and for preaching the gospel.

Q. But if He intended to console them, why did He speak in a way they did not understand?

A. Admire in this the loving solicitude of Jesus. To console one in affliction the most natural and most efficacious means is to draw the mind from the subject of one's sufferings, and this is done by occupying the mind with something else. He spoke to the apostles in this obscure manner to draw their attention from the sufferings which He foretold, and that He succeeded we see from the fact that they began to discuss His meaning and lost sight, for the time being, of those sufferings. Jesus also wished to convince them of His divinity, by showing them that He knew their thoughts.

Q. What do these words signify: "A little while, and you shall not see Me; and again a little while, and you shall see Me"?

A. According to the Jewish method of computing time, the day ended at sunset, when the following day began. Now while we say that the Last Supper took place on Thursday evening, according to the Jewish time it took place early on Friday, because it was after sunset on Thursday. Hence Christ's words, "A little while," etc., were said on the same day on which He was crucified. They would therefore see Him only a short time longer, because at three o'clock that day He would die on the cross. But as on the third day after His death He was to rise from the dead, they would see Him again. According to St. Augustine, these words, "A little while," mean the whole life-time, as if Christ meant to say that after a while He would go to the Father, and they would not see Him again until after their death, when they would see Him and share His joy and glory, of which no one could ever deprive them.

Q. How do you explain these words: "You shall lament and weep, but the world shall rejoice; and you shall be made sorrowful, but your sorrow shall be turned into joy"?

A. St. John Chrysostom says that Christ intended to say: "After a little while, nay, after a few hours, you will behold Me taken prisoner, tied, crucified, dead, and buried. And you, My disciples, will weep and mourn on account of what has befallen Me; and in the meantime My enemies will rejoice for having succeeded in overcoming Me. But after a little while, when I shall have risen gloriously from the grave, your sorrow will be changed into joy at beholding My triumph, and the rejoicing of My enemies will be turned into shame, disgrace, and despair." But St. Augustine, applying these words to the time we live on this earth, explains them as if Christ meant to say: "After My ascension into heaven you, My apostles, will weep and be sorrowful through preaching My law and the gospel, because you will be the target for the rage and enmity of the persecutors, and the worldlings will rejoice over your sufferings and your death; but after the short time that this world will last I shall come to judge the living and the dead, and then your sorrow will be turned into joy and eternal glory, and the insane rejoicings of the wicked will be changed into confusion, sorrow, and misery, which will never have an end."

Q. Are these words of Christ addressed to us?

A. They are, and to all good Christians, if we take them in the sense as explained by St. Augustine. The Divine Redeemer has positively declared that the cross is necessary for us, and that His faithful followers will weep and mourn in this world, and enjoy eternal happiness in heaven, so that all they suffered on earth will be turned into joy. St. Jerome says: "It is impossible for man to be happy both on earth and in heaven; it is impossible to enjoy the pleasures of this world and those of heaven; it is impossible to pass from the joys of the present life to the joys of life eternal." He who mourns on earth will rejoice in heaven, and he who laughs and is merry in the world will weep in hell.

Q. What did Christ wish to teach by the example of the woman who rejoices when the child is born?

A. Every child is the cause of great anxiety and labor to its mother; but she feels great joy and finds great delight in her child, she loves it tenderly, and would not give it for the whole world. Such was the joy the Divine Master promised His disciples after the great labors and sufferings of their apostolate. Jesus reigning gloriously in heaven was to be the reward of all their sufferings, the delight of their hearts, and their joy for all eternity.

Q. How can we apply all this to ourselves?

A. We must know that if we are faithful followers and true friends of Christ, we may expect sorrow, tribulations, and sufferings here on earth, but that all this will be for our greater glory and joy in heaven. We are now mourning like Joseph in the pit and in prison, but a day will come when our joy will be greater than his was when he was raised to the throne, and we will see that our humiliations and sufferings have been as so many steps by which we arrived at the height of happiness, and to the possession of a kingdom which no one can ever take from us.

FOURTH SUNDAY AFTER EASTER.

Gospel: St. John xvi. 5–14.

AT that time, Jesus said to His disciples: "I go to Him that sent Me, and none of you asketh Me: Whither goest Thou? But because I have spoken these things to you sorrow hath filled your heart. But I tell you the truth: it is expedient to you that I go, for if I go not, the Paraclete will not come to you; but if I go, I will send Him to you. And when He is come, He will convince the world of sin, and of justice, and of judgment. Of sin: because they believed not in Me. And of justice: because I go to the Father, and you shall see Me no longer. And of judgment: because the prince of this world is already judged. I have yet many things to say to you; but you cannot bear them now. But when He, the Spirit of truth, is come, He will teach you all truth; for He shall not speak of Himself, but what things soever He shall hear He shall speak, and the things that are to come He shall show you. He shall glorify Me, because He shall receive of Mine, and shall show it to you."

Q. Why did Jesus say to the apostles that He was going to the Father?

A. From the beginning of this discourse which He had with the apostles at the Last Supper, Christ had said that He was going away, but no one knew whither He was going, and no one asked Him. He, in thus speaking, wished them to understand that the time had come when He should leave them, because He was going to His crucifixion and death, after which, having proved His glorious resurrection by frequently appearing to them, He would be taken up before their eyes into heaven to sit at the right hand of His Father.

Q. Did Christ intend that the apostles should ask Him to tell in plain words where He was going?

A. Certainly. He wished them to ask Him whither He was going, because when they would hear that by means of His passion and death He would go to His glory and the possession of His kingdom, and when they would know the graces and recompenses He would obtain for them from His Father, they would be in great part consoled for their painful separation from Him.

Q. What did Christ say to His apostles that filled their hearts with sorrow?

A. Christ had just told them that He could remain with them but a short time, and they could not follow Him whither He was going; and now He announced to them that after His departure they would be persecuted, and their persecutors would imagine that they were serving God in putting them to death. The departure of their Master, and the prediction of the sufferings to which they were to be exposed, increased the sadness of their yet weak hearts.

Q. Did not Jesus console them?

A. He abundantly consoled them by adding: "I tell you the truth: it is expedient to you that I go;" as if He intended to say that they were equally mistaken if they felt sorry because He was about to leave them, inasmuch as it was for their own benefit, for He would send them the Holy Ghost, Who would not come if He did not ascend into heaven in order to send Him. To understand how consoling these words were to the apostles it is necessary to know that *Paraclete* means *Consoler*, and hence when Jesus promised them the Divine Paraclete they had nothing to fear on account of the absence of their Divine Master or the persecutions of their enemies.

Q. What sin was that of which the Holy Ghost would convince the world?

A. Our Divine Master indicated what this sin was by saying, "because they believed not in Me." In spite of all the proofs, the Jews did not acknowledge Jesus as the expected Messias, and the Gentiles did not even think of Him, nor had they so far accepted His doctrine. The Jews therefore sinned by their incredulity, their obstinacy, and their injustice, and these sins were the cause of many others, especially that of hatred, of envy, and of murder. The Gentiles on the other hand were engulfed in the mire of their passions without knowing their miserable condition. But after the Holy Ghost had bestowed His gifts on the apostles the world would know the injustice of the Jews and the guilt of the Gentiles; then the whole world would be convinced that Christ was truly the envoy sent by God, the Saviour of the world, the only One Who could lead us to eternal life.

Q. How was the Holy Ghost to convince the world of justice?

A. First of all, we must take the word justice in its true sense. Justice consists in the rectitude of the mind, in the innocence of the heart, and in the integrity of morals. He who always thinks of God, as he is strictly bound to do, whose affections are well regulated, loving, desiring what is good, fearing and avoiding what is evil, he who does good and not evil, he is, strictly speaking, a just man. Now we may judge whether the Jews and the Gentiles had this justice. The Gentiles professed false doctrines, they were corrupt in heart, and followed their passions, and therefore they regarded the religion of Christ as foolishness. The Jews, holding that sanctity consisted in the scrupulous observance of the legal ceremonies, persecuted the Envoy of heaven and believed they had gained great merit in the sight of God by putting Him to death. Now who was to undeceive both Jew and Gentile? Who was to teach them in what consisted true sanctity and true justice? Who was to give all creatures the tangible proofs of the sanctity, excellence, and greatness of Jesus Christ? It was the Holy Ghost; and the rapid and triumphant progress of the gospel is a proof thereof.

Q. Finally, how was the Holy Ghost to convince the world of judgment?

A. The Holy Ghost was to make known how false the judgment of the world was in regard to God, in regard to Christ, and in regard to the precepts of morality, because, as the Divine Master had said, the prince of this world was already judged, and was to be dethroned by the passion and death of the Redeemer. As soon as the apostles, filled with the Holy Ghost, preached the truths of the gospel, it was made known how deceived the Jews and Gentiles had been in their judgments; and the prince of the world, that is, the devil, who was the cause of such false judgments, finally lost that tyrannical power which up to that time he had exercised over their minds and hearts. Thus Christ a few hours before His death foretold that deliverance of men and that overthrow of the devil's power which the Holy Ghost accomplished after Pentecost.

Q. What did Christ mean when He said that He had many other things to tell them, but which they could not then understand?

A. We know very well how much the apostles did in founding the Church. They developed mysteries that are merely mentioned in the gospel, they fixed the discipline that was to be practised, they instituted the hierarchy of the clergy, determined the order of deacons, priests, and bishops, and founded the minor churches. We know also that when Christ thus spoke to them they were as yet ignorant, timid, and inconstant, and that by the power of the Holy Ghost they were to be transformed into new men. As long as they had not received the Holy Ghost they were not disposed to receive all the instructions necessary for so great an undertaking, and therefore Christ said that He had much more to tell them, but which they at present were not able to understand, and that the Holy Ghost would make it known to them.

Q. Why do you say this?

A. Consider the words that follow and you will no longer doubt it. The divine Redeemer said that when the Holy Ghost would come to the apostles He would teach them all truth, that is, He would tell them all that was to be done to establish the Church in the whole world. From this you see that Christ sent the Holy Ghost to instruct the apostles in all those things which on that evening they could not understand; and all which they afterward did and ordained in the Church of Christ was taught them by the Holy Ghost, Who constantly directed them in all things.

Q. What are we to learn from this Gospel?

A. Seeing the apostles filled with sorrow because they must separate from their divine Master, we should learn how great our sorrow ought to be when of our own accord we separate ourselves from Christ by sin; and learning how necessary the Holy Ghost was to the apostles, we should always invoke Him that He may also instruct us in the truths of the faith, and guide our steps on the way of evangelical perfection.

FIFTH SUNDAY AFTER EASTER.

Gospel: St. John xvi. 23–30.

AT that time, Jesus said to His disciples: "Amen, amen, I say to you: if you ask the Father anything in My name, He will give it you. Hitherto you have not asked anything in My name: Ask, and you shall receive, that your joy may be full. These things I have spoken to you in proverbs. The hour cometh when I will no more speak to you in proverbs, but will show you plainly of the Father. In that day you shall ask in My name: and I say not to you that I will ask the Father for you. For the Father Himself loveth you, because you have loved Me, and have believed that I came out from God. I came forth from the Father, and am come into the world: again I leave the world, and I go to the Father. His disciples say to Him: Behold now Thou speakest plainly, and speakest no proverb. Now we know that Thou knowest all things, and Thou needest not that any man should ask Thee. By this we believe that Thou comest forth from God."

Q. What did Christ promise the apostles in these words?

A. He promised the apostles, and all Christians, that His Eternal Father would grant them all graces when they ask for them in His name.

Q. Why may we hope to be always heard if we pray in the name of Jesus?

A. We know who Christ is, and what His merits are. He is the object of the complacency of the Father; He is the mediator between God and man; He it is upon Whom glory has been bestowed in preference to all creatures, because by His obedience and by His death He has merited the mercy, the adoption, and the benediction of the Father; and He has made us His brethren, His members, and co-heirs of His glory. The granting therefore of what we may ask of the Father in the name of Jesus will always be considered by Him as an act of mercy and grace toward us, and as an act of justice in regard to the infinite merits of Christ. Remember, however, that our prayers cannot be said to have been made in the name of Jesus when we ask for things that are not according to the spirit of Christ, and not expedient for our eternal welfare.

Q. If Christ made such a promise, why do we so often fail to receive what we ask for?

A. St. James the apostle says: "You ask and do not obtain because you ask amiss." St. Thomas says: "Some pray and at the same time are attached to sin, some do not pray as they ought, and some pray for things that are not good, or at least of no benefit to their soul, and therefore their prayers are not heard." If, however, they are sorry for their sins and pray in the proper manner for spiritual graces, and in the name of Jesus, the Eternal Father will grant their request.

Q. Why did Christ say that hitherto they had not asked in His name?

A. This is a matter of fact. The apostles were always with their Master, they looked to Him for what they wanted, and hence they never had recourse to the Eternal Father to obtain graces in His name. Now, Christ being about to leave them, He exhorts them henceforth to have recourse to His Father and pray to Him in His name, assuring them that on account of His merits the Father would hear their prayers, and console them in the trials of this world in which He was leaving them.

Q. Why does He say that hitherto He had spoken to them in proverbs?

A. The word "proverb" signifies a parable and also an enigma, and Jesus had hitherto made use of parables and enigmas in speaking to the apostles. You will recollect that He spoke to them in parables which they could not understand; even in the present discourse He said that after a little while they would not see Him, because He was going to the Father; that the Holy Spirit would come, and that their sorrow would be turned into joy; but all these words were to the apostles so many enigmas, the meaning of which they did not know. On this account He now promises them that He will henceforth speak to them in plain words by the voice of the Holy Ghost, and that nothing would be obscure or hard for them to understand. After Pentecost the apostles understood all, and spoke of the most sublime truths with wonderful clearness.

Q. What else did Christ promise?

A. He promised that the Holy Ghost would suggest to them what they should ask for, and that they would obtain their request from the Father without His being with them on earth; because the Eternal Father loved them on account of their faith in and love for Him, the Master. Let us love Him, and the Eternal Father will love us and will be always ready to hear our prayers.

Q. What did Christ mean when He said: "I came forth from the Father, and am come into the world; and I go to the Father"?

A. The Divine Word is generated by the Father before all ages, but in time He came into the world and assumed our own flesh. With that very same flesh He was, within a few days, to return to the Father, as His ascension into heaven was near at hand. Therefore with the above words He taught His divine generation, His incarnation, and His glorious ascension into heaven. The apostles understood all this and were confirmed in their faith, and hence they declared: "Behold now Thou speakest plainly. . . . By this we believe that Thou comest forth from God."

Q. What are we to learn from all this?

A. We should learn to grow in faith and in Christian hope; we should learn to pray in such a manner that our progress may be pleasing to the Eternal Father, so that we may obtain those graces for which we pray through Jesus Christ, in Jesus Christ, and with Jesus Christ.

SUNDAY WITHIN THE OCTAVE OF THE ASCENSION.

Gospel: St. John xv. 26-27; xvi. 1-4.

AT that time, Jesus said to His disciples: "When the Paraclete cometh Whom I will send you from the Father, the Spirit of truth, Who proceedeth from the Father, He shall give testimony of Me. And you shall give testimony, because you are with Me from the beginning. These things have I spoken to you, that you may not be scandalized. They will put you out of the synagogues: yea, the hour cometh that whosoever killeth you will think that he doth a service to God. And these things will they do to you, because they have not known the Father nor Me. But these things I have told you that when the hour of them shall come, you may remember that I told you."

Q. What did Christ promise here?

A. He promised that the Holy Ghost would give testimony of His divine mission, and of the truth of His doctrine. The promise was fulfilled. The world has acknowledged Jesus to be the only-begotten Word clothed with our flesh; it has recognized Him to be the Messias foretold by the prophets and foreshadowed in the law; it was convinced of the holiness of His doctrine, by which truths not known before were taught, and precepts inculcated worthy of the God Who taught them and worthy of man who was called to put them in practice with the help of divine grace.

Q. How were the apostles to give testimony of Jesus Christ?

A. The apostles were the first to know Him and to be intimately associated with Him; they were, therefore, witnesses of all He did and said. But, although they were constantly with Him, spoke with Him, saw all His actions, they did not always understand His words nor know the object of His actions. But after having received the Holy Ghost they remembered and understood all they had seen and heard during the three years of Christ's public life, and from all this they gathered the materials to teach the nations, to explain the truth, and to establish the discipline of that Church of which they were to be the founders throughout the world. They would preach to the nations the divinity of Christ and the truths of faith; they would say: We have heard with our own ears and seen with our own eyes all the things which we announce to you; and thus they would give testimony of Christ.

Q. Why did Christ say: "These things I have spoken to you, that you may not be scandalized"?

A. Christ sent the apostles to preach the gospel. Now what would they think of Him when they would find that they raised a most furious persecution against themselves, that they were everywhere hunted to death and abandoned to the fury of their enemies? They might have been tempted to believe that they had been betrayed and sacrificed by the Divine Master. Wherefore Christ told them all they would have to suffer, and by so doing He gave another proof of His divinity and also of His power to help them in the battles they were to fight in His name; and thus He anticipated and obviated all, in order that they might not lose their faith when those trials came upon them.

Q. What advantage did the apostles derive from these predictions?

A. St. Gregory says that a wound is less painful when it has been foreseen, and these predictions had this effect on the apostles, that the persecutions would be less painful, inasmuch as they expected them. Moreover, they would rejoice in the midst of those persecutions at beholding the predictions of their Divine Master fully verified, and the more their faith was strengthened the more they were encouraged by the hope of the reward which they were to gain by their sufferings.

Q. Were all these words intended only for the apostles?

A. In a certain sense they were also intended for us. We also bear witness to Jesus, by leading a life according to His holy law; we also, by sincerely professing the faith and by observing the laws of the gospel, may expect, as St. Paul says, to be persecuted; we also who find ourselves objects of persecution must be encouraged by the hope of our eternal reward in heaven.

PENTECOST SUNDAY.

Gospel: St. John xiv. 23–31.

AT that time, Jesus said to His disciples: "If any one love Me, he will keep My word, and My Father will love him, and We will come to him, and will make Our abode with him. He that loveth Me not, keepeth not My words. And the word which you have heard is not Mine: but the Father's Who sent Me. These things have I spoken to you, abiding with you. But the Paraclete, the Holy Ghost, Whom the Father will send in My name, He will teach you all things, and bring all things to your mind, whatsoever I shall have said to you. Peace I leave with you; My peace I give unto you: not as the world giveth do I give unto you. Let not your heart be troubled, nor let it be afraid. You have heard that I said to you: I go away and come again to you. If you loved Me, you would indeed be glad, because I go to the Father: for the Father is greater than I. And now I have told you before it came to pass: that when it shall come to pass you may believe. I will not now speak many things with you; for the prince of this world cometh, and in Me he hath not anything. But that the world may know that I love the Father: and as the Father hath given Me commandment, so do I. Arise, let us go hence."

Q. What does Jesus mean by the first words of this Gospel?

A. He tells those who sincerely love Him that they will show this love for Him by faithfully observing His precepts, and that in return for their love the Eternal Father will love them and, together with Himself and the Holy Ghost, will come to them, not only with His grace to preserve them in righteousness, to urge them to be perfect, to protect them and to enrich them with His blessings, but also to abide with them, to unite them to Himself, to make them a living temple of His divine majesty. Alas, our mind is too weak to understand the greatness of such a favor and of such a reward!

Q. How can you prove that he who loves not Christ does not keep His word?

A. A moment's reflection makes this evident. Look at those who love not Christ, and consider their conduct. Are they anxious to have Him for a friend, or do they appreciate what He has done for them? Do not many of them wish Him to be banished from the hearts of men? Are not even those who are not entirely wicked as indifferent toward Him as if He had never done anything for mankind? If you wish to know whether you love Christ, follow the advice of St. Gregory, and ask your own mind, tongue, and conduct. If you do not think of Him, if you do not speak of Him, if your manner of living is contrary to His law, you do not love Him.

Q. How are we to understand the other words relating to the Holy Ghost?

A. By these words Christ promised the apostles and His faithful followers that when He should leave this world and go to His Father, He would send the Holy Ghost, Who would be the teacher and consoler of the apostles and of all true Christians. The apostles had heard many things from Christ which they would fail to remember or could not understand. Hence the necessity of a teacher who would recall to their memory and assist them in understanding the things they had heard. Moreover, they were about to assume the arduous duties of the apostolate, they were to suffer all kinds of persecutions, and hence the promise of a comforter who would console them in all their afflictions. We all know the sublime manner in which these promises were fulfilled in reference to the apostles, and we all know, so far as we ourselves are concerned, that we cannot understand the profound meaning of the doctrines of Christ which we hear from the ministers of the Church unless the Holy Ghost be our teacher. And if in the trials of life we are patient and resigned, it is the gift of that Comforter Whom Christ promised us in the person of the Holy Ghost.

Q. What is that peace which Jesus Christ left us?

A. Consider Christ to have spoken thus: I am about to leave you, but I leave as an inheritance My benediction, by which I wish you every kind of good; not that apparent good which the world wishes you, but the good I wish you is real, efficacious, and fruitful unto all eternity. I leave you peace of mind, simplicity of heart, the bond of affection, charity, contentedness, courage, and the strength to acquire eternal glory, and to lead others to the same. Oh, what a consolation for us to know that these precious words did not stop with the apostles, but came down also directly to us!

Q. Why did He say that He would not speak many things with them, because the prince of this world was coming, who had no power over Him?

A. Do not forget that this discourse was held with the apostles on the evening before His passion. He therefore had only a few moments to speak to them. The horrible plan of His death had already been decided on by the synagogue, the devil was urging the

Jews to accomplish the crime, the traitor was at the head of the mob, yet neither the devil nor His enemies could have prevailed against Him, if He had not voluntarily given Himself up to them, in order to obey His Eternal Father. Therefore we see how Christ before He commenced His passion told the apostles what was to come, and how, in order to confirm His promise in regard to the Holy Ghost, He declared that He would suffer solely of His own accord and to do the will of His Eternal Father.

Q. When did Jesus fulfil His promise of sending the Holy Ghost?

A. The promise was fulfilled on Pentecost when suddenly there came a sound from heaven as of a mighty wind, and at the same time there appeared cleft tongues, as it were, of fire, that rested on each one of the disciples, who for several days had been together in a room praying.

Q. Why did the Holy Ghost come down upon the apostles in this manner?

A. The Holy Ghost did so in order to manifest Himself in a visible manner, for, says St. Gregory of Nazianzen, if the Divine Word assumed a real body and thus lived among us, it was proper that the Holy Ghost should also manifest Himself to man in a visible manner.

Q. But why did He manifest Himself in the form of fiery tongues, and why was His coming preceded by a strong wind?

A. The Holy Ghost has always assumed different forms according to the nature of His works. When Christ was baptized in the river Jordan He appeared in the form of a dove, which is innocent, fruitful, and the bearer of peace, in order to signify Christ's innocence, the object of His mission, and the fruitfulness of His works. He appeared at the transfiguration of Christ on Mt. Thabor in the form of a resplendent cloud covering the Redeemer, Moses, Elias, the apostles, and the summit of the mountain, to indicate that He directed the prophets, the law, Christ, and the apostles, and that He protects and renders the Church fruitful. Lastly, He appeared on Pentecost under a new form, which clearly indicated the wonders of which He was the worker.

Q. What did the strong wind and the fiery tongues signify?

A. The strong wind signified the power and the energy with which the Holy Ghost came upon the apostles, in order to render them strong, active, and courageous in attacking, fighting, and conquering the world; the fire signified that ardor of charity which was to purify, enlighten, inflame, and raise the mind and heart of man to heaven; the tongues signified that divine science, triumphant eloquence; and knowledge of all languages, of which the apostles would make so great use in converting the world.

Q. What were the effects of the descent of the Holy Ghost upon the apostles?

A. The principal effects were: The apostles were full of imperfections, and the Holy Ghost made them saints, that henceforth in all their thoughts, desires, affections, words, actions, and endeavors they were moved by God, they sought God, and referred themselves to God. They were ignorant, and now they knew all the mysteries, and they cited and explained the Holy Scriptures; they established the deposit of truth; and they became the teachers of the Catholic faith. They were timid and apprehensive, and from that moment they were courageous and brave, so that they feared not the cruelty of tyrants. We can say with St. Gregory: Behold that Peter rejoicing at the sound of the scourge who before trembled at a word; and he who was frightened at the voice of a servant girl, having received the Holy Ghost, smiles in the tyrant's face who has caused his shoulders to be torn.

Q. What are we to do on this day?

A. We should admire and adore the power of the Holy Ghost, and beseech Him to renew His wonders in our souls, and render thanks to God Who, on that day and in such manner, accomplished the mysteries of the faith and the establishment of His holy Church.

FIRST SUNDAY AFTER PENTECOST, OR TRINITY SUNDAY.

Gospel: St. Luke vi. 36-42.

AT that time, Jesus said to His disciples: "Be ye merciful, as your Father also is merciful. Judge not, and you shall not be judged: condemn not, and you shall not be condemned. Forgive, and you shall be forgiven. Give, and it shall be given to you: good measure and pressed down and shaken together and running over shall they give into your bosom. For with the same measure that you shall mete withal, it shall be measured to you again. And He spoke also to them a similitude: Can the blind lead the blind? do they not both fall into the ditch? The disciple is not above his master; but every one shall be perfect, if he be as his master. And why seest thou the mote in thy brother's eye, but the beam that is in thy own eye thou considerest not? Or how canst thou say to thy brother: Brother, let me pull the mote out of thy eye, when thou thyself seest not the beam in thy own eye. Hypocrite, cast first the beam out of thy own eye, and then shalt thou see clearly to take out the mote from thy brother's eye."

Q. What does Christ exhort us to do in this Gospel?

A. After having commanded His disciples, and in their person us also, to be as perfect as the Heavenly Father, He makes known to them that the first step to take to be so is to be charitable toward our neighbor, as God is full of charity toward us. The object of the whole discourse is to commend the principal works of mercy, and to censure that pride and false piety which causes us to see the faults of our neighbor but not our own, and thus to have no mercy for our neighbor.

Q. Which are the principal works of mercy commanded in this Gospel?

A. The first is not to judge others rashly; the second is not to condemn him who has fallen; the third is to pardon him who has offended us; and the fourth is to give alms or in other ways help those who need our help.

Q. Is it a sin to judge the actions of others?

A. The Holy Ghost tells us not to trouble ourselves with things that do not concern us. If, therefore, our neighbor does something that is not praiseworthy, as long as it does not interfere with our affairs and our conscience, charity commands us to close our eyes and not take notice of it. Charity much more forbids us to judge our neighbors' actions upon grounds that are insufficient and more imaginary than real. Hence Christ in this passage of the Gospel commands us not to judge rashly of our neighbors' actions; that is, without having positive reasons. However, let us reflect that if, judging from appearances, the conduct of our neighbor is not praiseworthy, then we can and should be on our guard and avoid all intercourse with him, so that our reputation and conscience may not suffer.

Q. Is it against charity to condemn any one who sins?

A. St. Bernard says: When the failings of your brother cannot be denied, excuse the intention, attribute them to ignorance or surprise; have compassion on his weakness, and think that you might have done the very same under similar circumstances. This is the law of charity. Some one has said a word that is positively bad; are we sure that he knew the full meaning of it? Another has done something that is not very good; are we sure that he did it intentionally and with reflection? Again, one has given way to a fit of anger; do we know whether, under the circumstances, he had time to repress the passion? Another's sin is evident; but would we under similar circumstances have been more faithful to God? Charity commands us to excuse our brethren, and Jesus Christ gives us this command in this day's Gospel.

Q. What are we to think of the other suggestion in which He tells us to pardon?

A. It is a most just, holy, and wholesome suggestion. The Pharisees had brought a woman to Christ who had been caught in actual sin, and according to the law she should be stoned to death. Jesus wrote some words on the ground and then said. "He that is without sin among you let him first cast a stone" (John viii. 7). We may very appropriately apply these words to ourselves. He that needs no pardon from God may refuse to pardon his neighbor. God will forgive us in the same degree that we forgive others. How just, holy, and beneficial is not, therefore, the command Christ gives us here.

Q. Why are we to give to others what belongs to us?

A. Mark well that by the words of Christ we are bound in charity to give to others only what is superfluous to us. Whatever is not necessary for us, according to our state in life, is not our own, but God's, Who gives it to us so that we may gain merit by giving it to the poor. If we were in want, what would our wish be? Certainly that others would have compassion on us and help us. Therefore charity requires that we do for others what we wish for ourselves. Hence, if our neighbor be in want we must help him by giving him as alms what is superfluous to us, or we must at least lend him what we do not need.

Q. What reward does Christ promise us for all this?

A. If we close our eyes in order not to see the faults of our neighbor, God will mercifully close His eyes to ours. If we do not judge, but rather have compassion on others, God will not judge, He will compassionate our failings. If we pardon our neighbor, God will pardon us; and if we give charity to the needy, God will give us the treasures of His grace. In a word, as we treat our neighbor God will treat us, with this difference, however, that we do good to others as men whose power is limited, whereas God will favor us with a power that is infinite, and with a generosity altogether His own.

Q. What are the vices that prevent us from doing the above works of charity?

A. They are pride and false piety, that is, hypocrisy. The proud man thinks he knows all, sees all, and whatever he does he does well. Therefore as a king he condemns all those who do not act as he does; ordinarily speaking, he is cruel, he does not forgive, and never gives alms. The hypocrites are extremely severe with others whilst they are exceedingly indulgent to themselves, and therefore you will look in vain for Christian charity in the proud or in the hypocrite. They fancy themselves full of good works, whereas in reality they are like clouds in summer that pass away without letting a drop of rain fall upon the parched earth.

Q. What lesson are we to learn from the words "the blind cannot lead the blind"?

A. We are to learn that we should not assume charge of others, if we have not sufficient knowledge to properly discharge our duty; besides, we should trust only those who, on account of their probity and knowledge, deserve our confidence. An ignorant, immoral, and worldly counsellor can but drag our soul after him into the abyss.

Q. Who are they who see the mote in their brother's eye, but see not the beam in their own?

A. They are those false devotees and proud people who notice the most trifling faults of their neighbor, and care not about their own misdeeds and sins. Christ tells these they should first correct their own wicked ways before they presume to correct others;

and hence, if we wish to avoid the reproach of the Divine Master, we must pay attention to our own failings, and not busy ourselves with our neighbors' unless duty or charity should command it.

SECOND SUNDAY AFTER PENTECOST.

Gospel: St. Luke xiv. 16–24.

AT that time, Jesus spoke to the Pharisees this parable: "A certain man made a great supper, and invited many. And he sent his servant at the hour of supper to say to them that were invited that they should come, for now all things are ready. And they began all at once to make excuse. The first said to him: I have bought a farm, and I must needs go out and see it: I pray thee, hold me excused. And another said· I have bought five yoke of oxen, and I go to try them: I pray thee, hold me excused. And another said: I have married a wife, and therefore I cannot come. And the servant returning told these things to his lord. Then the master of the house, being angry, said to his servant: Go out quickly into the streets and lanes of the city, and bring in hither the poor and the feeble and the blind and the lame. And the servant said: Lord, it is done as thou hast commanded, and yet there is room. And the lord said to the servant: Go out into the highways and hedges; and compel them to come in, that my house may be filled. But I say unto you, that none of those men that were invited shall taste of my supper."

Q. Who is this man who prepares the supper, and what supper is it that is called great?

A. All agree that this man is our good God, Who places His treasures at the disposal of His friends, that is, our souls, and invites His creatures to nourish themselves at His heavenly banquet, which is replenished with all sweetness and delights. In regard to the supper we must, first of all, observe that dinner and supper are different in this: that work is stopped to take dinner, and after, the work is generally resumed, and man is once more taken up with the cares and anxieties of life; but after supper he works no more, he retires to rest, and in the sweet embraces of sleep he forgets all that afflicts his mind and body. Hence all the sacred interpreters say that the nuptial banquet or the dinner mentioned in the eighth chapter of St. Matthew, signifies the vocation to the faith, after which there is much work to be done, and much to suffer in the practice of the Christian life. The supper, however, mentioned in this day's Gospel signifies the entrance into paradise, after which there is perfect peace and rest, and nothing to disturb the mind or tire the body. Many, however, recognize in this supper the holy Eucharistic table, and that most precious food that is taken by receiving the Most Holy Sacrament.

Q. In what does the supper resemble the Most Holy Eucharist?

A. When the hour for supper has come the work or business of the day is done, the meal is taken in peace, the time is passed in pleasant conversation, and then each retires to rest, during which the tired body recovers new strength, the mind gains new vigor, and upon rising the following morning all feel refreshed and able to resume their work. Now the same happens to the soul when it partakes of the Eucharistic table. When a Christian approaches this table with the proper dispositions he forgets entirely the cares of the world, he converses confidentially with God, his true friend, brother, and father; he enjoys peace of mind, during which he recovers from all his sufferings; he receives new strength to battle against his spiritual enemies and to carry even heavier crosses, and, like a new man, he attempts to climb the high mountain of evangelical perfection.

Q. Of whom are they who refused to come to the supper a figure?

A. They are the figure of the Christians who, being immersed in the cares, pleasures, and vanities of the world, do not care to receive the Holy Sacrament, and do not prepare themselves to enter into the heavenly rest, thus showing by their actions that they refuse to be of the number of the elect.

Q. And of whom are the poor, the feeble, the blind, and the lame that were invited to the supper a figure?

A. From this we learn that God, in bestowing His favors, has no regard for high birth, riches, talents, beauty, or other personal advantages; so much so that the poor and lowly are treated kindly by Him, and sometimes even better than the great of the world. It is not only the perfect that are called to nourish themselves at the Eucharistic table, but also those who are poor in merits, blind according to the spirit, ignorant and less constant in the divine service; for by virtue of this heavenly bread they will become rich in grace, gain strength, be enlightened, and be rendered able to make greater progress in virtue. Let timid souls impress this lesson of the parable on their minds, and draw therefrom comfort and consolation.

Q. What are we to say of the master of the house who was angry at those who excused themselves?

A. Woe to those who do not heed God's invitation! A day will come when they will no more hear that voice inviting them to taste the delights of paradise. The Jews, of whom those who refused to attend the supper were a figure, did not heed the words of the Divine Master, and they were abandoned to their sad fate. All who resist the voice of God, Who calls them to eternal happiness in so many different ways, will find that they are excluded therefrom. As we have applied the parable to the Blessed Sacrament, let us reflect that he who, on account of worldly cares or of a sinful life, does not receive this sacrament runs the greatest risk of being deprived of it at the hour of death, because then Jesus Christ will refuse to be the food of those ungrateful ones who turned away from Him when He most lovingly invited them during life to partake of His table.

THIRD SUNDAY AFTER PENTECOST.

Gospel: St. Luke xv. 1-10.

AT that time: "The publicans and sinners drew near unto Jesus to hear Him. And the Pharisees and the scribes murmured, saying: This man receiveth sinners and eateth with them. And He spoke to them this parable, saying: What man of you that hath an hundred sheep, and if he shall lose one of them, doth he not leave the ninety-nine in the desert, and go after that which was lost until he find it? And when he hath found it, lay it upon his shoulders rejoicing, and coming home call together his friends and neighbors, saying to them: Rejoice with me, because I have found my sheep that was lost? I say to you, that even so there shall be joy in heaven upon one sinner that doth penance, more than upon ninety-nine just who need not penance. Or what woman having ten groats, if she lose one groat, doth not light a candle and sweep the house and seek diligently until she find it? And when she hath found it, call together her friends and neighbors, saying: Rejoice with me, because I have found the groat which I had lost. So I say to you, there shall be joy before the angels of God upon one sinner doing penance."

Q. What are we to think of those sinners who gathered about Christ, and of Him Who received them?

A. We are to admire the goodness of the Divine Redeemer, and it would be well if all Christians would imitate those publicans. They heard, as we read in St. Matthew, that the divine Redeemer invited all to do penance because the kingdom of heaven was nigh, and therefore they came to Him and they were well received. Happy they who voluntarily go to hear the doctrine of Christ preached by His ministers! This is, generally speaking, the first step toward repentance and perfection. The internal inspirations and the impulses of our heart which we experience in hearing the word of God are a proof of the kind welcome which Jesus Christ is accustomed to give us.

Q. Why did the Pharisees and scribes murmur?

A. They did not know, or, rather, did not wish to know, that a truly just man always feels compassion for sinners, and that the saints have always desired and endeavored to promote their conversion and eternal welfare. The proud and hypocritical Pharisees avoided public sinners, as if they would have been contaminated by permitting sinners to come near to them, and they wanted Jesus Christ to do as they did; but as He received them kindly, they were angry and murmured. Let us learn from the Divine Master to be charitable toward him who errs, and let us avoid the pride and hard-heartedness of the Pharisees.

Q. What is the object of this parable?

A. By this parable Christ wished to excuse sinners, He desired to encourage them to be converted, and to let them know how dear they are to the most merciful God, Who goes in search of the lost, Who helps them with His grace in their repentance, and Who rejoices with His angels in heaven when they return to the path that leads to salvation.

Q. Where do we find excuse for sinners?

A. We find it in the parable where Christ compares a sinner to a sheep. The sheep is a very simple and dull animal which, while grazing in the field, does not notice that it has left the fold. It is lost, and when lost does not know the way back to the fold. It seems, therefore, that when Christ compared the sinner to a sheep He intended to say that the sinner goes astray from the true path and from God through pure and natural ignorance; because, being dazzled and delighted by the things of the world, he follows them; he separates himself from the just without knowing it, and, lost in the desert of this world, he does not know his misfortune and has not, humanly speaking, the means of returning again, if God in His infinite mercy does not go in search of him and rescues him.

Q. Where do we find encouragement for sinners?

A. We find it where Christ compares Himself to the shepherd by pointing out his labors and conduct. From the words of the Divine Master we see that as soon as the shepherd missed the lost sheep he hastened after it, and when he found it he did not frighten it with reproaches, nor punish it, nor compel it to walk; but, calling it by name, he folds it in his arms, and pitying its weariness, he carries it on his shoulders to the fold, and calls his friends together to rejoice with him for having brought back to the fold an unfortunate one which was in danger of being devoured by the wolves. What greater encouragement is there for the sinner who sees in the lost sheep his own condition and in the conduct of the shepherd the infinite mercy of God?

Q. Can you show me in Christ what we have seen in the shepherd?

A. As the shepherd immediately searches for the sheep when he knows it is lost, so God immediately recalled Adam to the right path when he had lost it by sin, by announcing to him the fruit of the woman, that is, the Saviour, Who was to crush the head of the serpent. The shepherd leaves the ninety-nine in order to seek the lost sheep; and the Divine Word, in order to save Adam and his race, left the company of the angels and the splendor of His glory, and came to dwell on earth under the likeness of a servant. The shepherd, having found the sheep, treats it kindly; and the God-man, when he was among sinners, treated them with ineffable tenderness, and out of kindness for them worked many miracles. The shepherd carried the sheep on his shoulders, and the God-man carried us on His shoulders, and alone sustained the weight of our sins. And as the shepherd called his friends to rejoice with him because he had found the lost sheep, so the Incarnate Word called all the angels to rejoice with Him, when from Mount Olivet He returned triumphantly to His Father, taking with Him those of the human race whom He had rescued from hell.

Q. Can it be said that the same occurs in the conversion of every sinner?

A. When we consider the great remorse the sinner feels after having committed sin, the interior voice that calls him to repent, the charity with which the priest, by the command of Jesus Christ, must receive him, the consolation the heart of a true penitent experiences when receiving absolution, the light, the help, and the graces that assist him to return to the right path, and to reform his life, the joy of the angels and saints at his conversion, we will understand that God always goes in search of the erring, that He treats them with kindness, that He supports them by His grace, and that He rejoices at their return to Him.

Q. What is the meaning of the other parable—of the woman who seeks the lost groat?

A. St. Gregory in his thirty-fourth homily says that the woman signifies the Divine Wisdom. The coin which bears the image of the king is a figure of a soul which bears the image of the Creator. The loss of the groat is a figure of the fall of man, and the light announces the incarnation of the Word, because as the light shines through the lamp, so the divinity of Christ shone through His humanity. The sweeping and seeking through the house signifies the Incarnate Wisdom that aroused the consciences of men who were living tranquilly in their sins, and freed them from their errors of intellect and from the corruption of their hearts. When the groat was found, our soul, made according to the likeness of God, was redeemed and placed on the way of salvation; and then the Infinite Wisdom called justice, mercy, omnipotence, providence, and all the heavenly powers to rejoice with it. Thus we see that the shepherd and the woman are figures of Jesus Christ, as the sheep and the groat are figures of the sinner.

Q. Why did the Divine Master conclude by saying that there shall be more joy for one repentant sinner than for ninety-nine just who need not penance?

A. St. Gregory sees in the nine groats, and St. Ambrose in the ninety-nine sheep, the nine heavenly hierarchies and the countless choirs of angels who are happy in eternal bliss; and in the one lost sheep and one lost groat they behold the human race lost by sin. And the salvation of man, which is of so great advantage to man himself, the cause of so great joy to the angels, and of so great glory to God, produced unheard-of rejoicing in heaven, not because God loved the heavenly spirits less, but because man had been restored to eternal life which he had lost by sin. Now, in the conversion of each sinner the accidental joy of paradise is increased; because, although it is perfect, yet it is increased when a soul is rescued from hell and restored to God.

Q. What are we to learn from all this?

A. Besides understanding the sense and the spirit of the parable and the object the Divine Master had in view in telling it, we are to learn to be charitable toward sinners, to be zealous for their conversion, to be anxious in working out our own conversion, if such be our need, and always to thank Our Lord Jesus Christ, Who in His infinite mercy came in search of us when we were in the state of perdition.

FOURTH SUNDAY AFTER PENTECOST.

Gospel: St. Luke v. 1-11.

AT that time: "When the multitude pressed upon Jesus to hear the word of God, He stood by the Lake of Genesareth, and saw two ships standing by the lake, but the fishermen were gone out of them and were washing their nets. And going up into one of the ships that was Simon's, He desired him to draw back a little from the land. And sitting He taught the multitude out of the ship. Now when He had ceased to speak He said to Simon: Launch out into the deep, and let down your nets for a draught. And Simon answering said to Him: Master, we have labored all the night, and have taken nothing, but at Thy word I will let down the net. And when they had done this they enclosed a very great multitude of fishes, and their net broke. And they beckoned to their partners that were in the other ship that they should come and help them. And they came and filled both the ships, so that they were almost sinking: which, when Simon Peter saw, he fell down at Jesus' knees, saying: Depart from me, for I am a sinful man, O Lord. For he was wholly astonished, and all that were with him, at the draught of the fishes which they had taken. And so were also James and John, the sons of Zebedee, who were Simon's partners. And Jesus saith to Simon: Fear not; from henceforth thou shalt catch men. And having brought their ships to land, leaving all things, they followed Him."

Q. Of what is this ship a figure?

A. This ship belonged to St. Peter, and St. Ambrose says that it is the same which St. Matthew speaks of as tossed about by a furious tempest, and St. Luke in this day's Gospel describes as overloaded with fishes. From this ship Christ taught the people; from it He commanded the wind and the waves; from it, although asleep, He saved the apostles from drowning. It is, therefore, a figure of the Catholic Church, of which St. Peter and his legitimate successors are the visible head and foundation.

Q. How do you compare the Catholic Church to the bark of Peter?

A. The Catholic Church has been exposed from her very beginning to the persecutions of paganism, heresy, and false philosophy. By the preaching of the apostles and their successors she has made immense conquests in all parts of the world. In the midst of continual vicissitudes she has always had the assistance of God, Who watched over her safety and led her to victory, although He seemed to sleep and to have abandoned her to the fury of her enemies. She possesses the truth, and teaches heavenly doctrines that are directly opposed to the spirit of the world. You will, therefore, recognize in her the bark of Peter, now tossed about by the waves, now loaded with rich treasures, now triumphing over the tempests, because Jesus Christ is with her, and as the oracle of her Master she teaches whomsoever listens to her from the shore.

Q. Is there any remark to be made about the order He gave the apostles to launch out into the deep and to let down their nets, after He had ceased to speak?

A. To launch out into the deep signified the great work into which the apostles were to go; and to let down their nets indicated the preaching of the divine word by which they were to draw all the nations of the earth from the abyss of ignorance and place them in the bosom of the Church. It was, therefore, necessary that Jesus Christ should first teach and finish His teaching, since the apostles and their successors would have to repeat His very words; and, when He had fully revealed the truth, He sent His apostles to preach it to the whole world. Observe, however, that if the apostles preached the gospel, they did so by the command of Jesus Christ; therefore, no one can ever pretend to have the right of preaching the gospel unless he has received his mission from the legitimate successors of the apostles who are in union with their head, the vicar of Jesus Christ.

Q. What is to be said of the answer of St. Peter?

A. Peter answered: "Master, we have labored all night and have taken nothing, but at Thy word I will let down the net." In the first place we observe that we shall always labor in vain if we are not in the company of Jesus with His grace. He who does not work for God and with God loses his time, and gains nothing; he may gain for the world but not for heaven. Therefore, we shall be indeed unfortunate if, at the end of our lives, after having done so much for the world, we find that we have gained nothing for eternity. We admire the obedience of St. Peter, who, although the time was not favorable, let down his net at the word of his Master; and we also should obey him who commands us in God's place, whatever reasons we may have for doing the contrary.

Q. What is meant by the danger of the net breaking?

A. There is always danger in a crowd, and after the whole world wanted to enter the Church and be called Christian, the fervor of the faith was diminished. The weak in the faith, the disobedient sinners, continually threaten to break the mystical net; that is, the effect of the word of God. And heretics, schismatics, and false Christians do break it.

Q. What are we to say of their calling their partners to help them?

A. We are to learn from this that when we are not strong enough to do what is required of us it is not sufficient to confess our inability, but we must moreover ask those to help us who can do so. A father of a family, a teacher, a high official, must always ask for the help or advice of competent persons, when they cannot alone properly discharge their duties toward those committed to their care.

Q. What are we to say of the great number of fishes which they caught?

A. It was a figure of the most fruitful result of the work of the apostles, who, by their preaching, gained in a very short time to the faith a great multitude of persons of every age, class, and nation. At the same time we also learn how fruitful our works will be if God is near to us with His grace, and if we undertake a work in obedience to His word; for if St. Peter, who had worked all night in vain, by obeying his Divine Master caught so great a number of fishes, our gain will also be very great for eternity if we act through obedience.

Q. Why did Christ permit the apostles to be so astonished at what had happened?

A. This was a very extraordinary grace, of which all stand in need who attribute everything to chance or to natural causes, and never recognize and adore the manifest working of the hand of God, not even in the most extraordinary events. Besides, it was a lesson to those obstinate unbelievers who, knowing the rich and prodigious spiritual draught effected by the apostles by preaching the gospel, still refuse to acknowledge the truth and to confess the divinity of the Catholic religion, which has so often been proved beyond all doubt.

Q. What are we to learn from the events recorded in this Gospel?

A. We are to learn from the multitude to be anxious to hear the word of God. From St. Peter we are to learn to obey Jesus Christ, and to humble ourselves, having our unworthiness before our eyes, when God favors us and makes us the instruments of His wonders. From the apostles, who abandoned their ships and nets, we are to learn to abandon the things of the world, to give up our affections, even our own selves, in order to follow the voice of God when He vouchsafes to call us. Since Jesus Christ has sufficiently instructed the world, He has in a certain sense finished His discourse, so far as we are concerned; let us, therefore, launch out into the deep; let us work, and, disengaging our hearts from the world, follow our Master on the way to heaven.

FIFTH SUNDAY AFTER PENTECOST.

Gospel: St. Matthew v. 20-24.

AT that time, Jesus said to His disciples: "For I tell you, that unless your justice abound more than that of the scribes and Pharisees you shall not enter into the kingdom of heaven. You have heard that it was said to them of old: Thou shalt not kill, and whosoever shall kill shall be in danger of the judgment. But I say to you, that whosoever is angry with his brother shall be in danger of the judgment. And whosoever shall say to his brother, Raca, shall be in danger of the council. And whosoever shall say, Thou fool, shall be in danger of hell-fire. If therefore thou offer thy gift at the altar, and there thou remember that thy brother hath anything against thee, leave there thy offering before the altar, and go first to be reconciled to thy brother; and then coming thou shalt offer thy gift."

Q. What did Christ mean by the first words of this Gospel?

A. He meant to teach the apostles, and all future Christians, that in order to enter into the kingdom of heaven it is necessary to be more just and holy than the Pharisees claimed to be. The people thought the Pharisees were holy and most just men, but their justice and sanctity was only apparent and superficial. They were very exact in the observance of the external ceremonies, of the ablutions, and in paying the tithes; but they cared not about the interior vices of the heart, and while they appeared to be immaculate, they were full of malice and corruption. Hence, Christ said that, in order to enter into the kingdom of heaven, it was necessary to be more holy than the Pharisees; that is, to be holy in fact, and not merely in appearance.

Q. And what did He mean by the words that follow?

A. He intended to explain fully and to perfect the commandment that forbids homicide, by forbidding internal feelings of anger, reproachful words, and contempt, which, like so many steps, lead to the killing of our neighbor, endeavoring thus to prevent the violation of that commandment in its very birth.

Q. How are we to understand these words: " Whosoever is angry with his brother shall be in danger of the judgment"?

A. We are to understand that every act and every feeling of anger against our neighbor, whether for a grave or slight matter, will be judged by God as deserving of punishment, and that He will punish it according to its degree of malice.

Q. How do you explain the other words?

A. The word *Raca*, according to St. Jerome, is a Hebrew or Syriac word, which means the same as simpleton, one good for nothing, etc. Everybody knows that such reproachful words are the first expressions of anger which go to increase the anger, and which are greater sins than the merely internal emotion of anger. Hence Christ says that he who offends his neighbor by such words shall be summoned before the council, that is, the sanhedrim, composed of the senators of the people, to be sentenced according to his guilt; which, after mature deliberation, they do according to the greater or lesser malice of the culprit. Let us learn from this that God will judge the words we utter against our neighbor; that He will weigh all the circumstances; that is, whether we uttered such words inadvertently or purposely, whether we were taken by surprise or not; He will take into consideration who the offended person is, and who the culprit; and, according to the malice, God will sentence the sinner to the punishment he deserves, either temporal or eternal.

Q. Explain these words: "Whosoever shall say to his brother, thou fool, shall be guilty of hell-fire."

A. According to St. Jerome, Christ intended to say *hell*, when He said fire of Gehenna, that is, the fiercest fire; and He declared him guilty of hell who in anger would say to his brother, thou fool. However, by this parable are understood all those insults or acts of contempt which grievously dishonor our neighbor; so that if it be a grievous sin to call another a fool, it is much more so to call him a thief, an impostor, or libertine, which is so often done.

Q. What does Christ further command us to do?

A. He commands us to be reconciled to our neighbor whom we have offended as soon as possible, and to give him satisfaction. The Jews thought they could atone for any sin, even for murder, by making an offering in the temple; and Jesus Christ commanded them not to make the offering until they had made peace with their neighbor, which they should do immediately. We, also, are bound by this command; and hence, if we have either in word or deed offended a person, before we pray or receive the sacraments we should banish from our heart all angry feeling; we should, as soon as possible, give satisfaction and ask pardon of the person offended; and we should show that we entertain no feelings of resentment, and if we have been offended we must be ready to forgive.

Q. What are we to learn from this Gospel?

A. We are to learn that to enter into the kingdom of heaven we must be really and not apparently good; that is, we must have an upright heart animated by charity and subject in all things to the holy law of God, always bearing in mind that true justice does not consist in the external practices of devotion, but rather in the purity of conscience, in the abnegation of our will, and in the control of our passions. We are also to learn to abstain from any act of anger, and from saying anything that can offend or grieve our neighbor. Lastly, we are to learn not to be slow in making peace with our neighbor whenever we have displeased him, and also not to make a reconciliation difficult.

SIXTH SUNDAY AFTER PENTECOST.

Gospel: St. Mark viii. 1-9.

AT that time: "When there was a great multitude, and they had nothing to eat, calling His disciples together, He saith to them: I have compassion on the multitude, for behold they have now been with Me three days and have nothing to eat. And if I shall send them away fasting to their home they will faint in the way, for some of them came from afar off. And His disciples answered Him: From whence can any one fill them here with bread, in the wilderness? And He asked them: How many loaves have ye? Who said: seven. And He commanded the multitude to sit down upon the ground. And taking the seven loaves, giving thanks, He broke, and gave to His disciples to set before them, and they set them before the people. And they had a few little fishes; and He blessed them, and commanded them to be set before them. And they did eat, and were filled, and they took up that which was left of the fragments, seven baskets. And they that had eaten were about four thousand: and He sent them away."

Q. Of whom is this multitude a figure?

A. It may be said in the first place to be a figure of all those who lived before Christ. In the second place it was a figure of the Jewish people, and lastly of the Gentiles. The first could not behold Christ, the Saviour, Whom they so ardently expected. The Jews had only figures, shadows, and carnal victims, which could not nourish their souls; and the Gentiles were dying of hunger, because they had nothing but prejudices, evil habits, and vices that were leading them to perdition. Happy are we who have received the bread of life which nourishes, strengthens, and sanctifies our souls in the desert of this world!

Q. And those who came from afar, of whom are they a figure?

A. They are a figure of the Gentiles. The Jews, by the vocation of Abraham and by the law of Moses, were on the way to meet the Saviour, and were very near to Him, because He was to be born in their midst. The Gentiles, on the contrary, were far from Him, because their ignorance, their superstitions, and their immoralities made them strangers to God and placed them out of the way of salvation. Yet they also came to hear Christ, they enjoyed the effects of His mercy, they were fed with His doctrine, and were nourished with the food of life. As to ourselves, however, those persons who came from afar off represent those sinners who, like the prodigal son, go to a distant country, that is, far from their heavenly home, following their passions, and they come, indeed, from afar off when they come to hear the word of God, by means of which they find God disposed to have compassion on them, and to feed them with the bread of His grace and to provide for them, that they may not grow faint on the road they still have to walk in the exercise of penance. What a consolation for poor sinners!

Q. What is to be said of the compassion of Jesus Christ?

A. We are to admire the greatness of His love for our souls. We live on this earth as in the midst of a desert, where there is nothing that will satisfy our souls. But Jesus Christ does not forget our misery; He knows even our least wants; He has a most tender compassion for us, and He provides abundantly for us.

Q. How do you infer this from the Gospel?

A. Because Jesus Christ, as St. Gregory says, taught sometimes by word of mouth and sometimes by His actions. Hence in all that He did to the multitude in this day's Gospel we see what He continually does in our souls. Following the Gospel, we see Jesus in the midst of the people, who crowd around Him; He notices how pale and weak they are; He sees the effects of their fast; He is moved at such a sight, and consults with His apostles about supplying food for so great a multitude. He causes the little they had taken with them for their own use to be placed before Him, and had the apostles distribute it with the utmost impartiality, giving so abundantly that seven baskets of fragments remained. Now, according to the teachings of faith, we should see Jesus ever watching over our souls, weighing and measuring the needs of each one, having pity for all and giving forth to all His doctrines, His light, His graces, His sacraments, His body, and His merits. All this He does by the ministry of His priests, without regard to person, sex, or age, and provides all with abundant means to live faithful to Him in this world and happy with Him in the next.

Q. What do the seven loaves signify?

A. According to the sacred interpreters they signify the seven gifts of the Holy Ghost, which our Divine Saviour makes use of to preserve the life of our soul, strengthening it to walk in the midst of dangers, to overcome the temptations, and to grow in virtue and Christian perfection.

Q. And what did the little fishes signify?

A. Those fishes served to render the bread more agreeable to the taste, and they signify all that which renders easier the observance of the divine word, which is the ordinary food of our soul. The example of Jesus Christ, Who practised all the precepts which He gave us in His holy law, the lights which our mind receives, the joy our heart feels in doing good, the confidence that supports us in leading a Christian life in the midst of difficulties—these are the exquisite food which renders the observance of the commandments easy and pleasant to us.

Q. What are we to do to make good use of these spiritual nourishments?

A. To make good use of these spiritual nourishments we must pray God to give and preserve in us the gift of His habitual grace; we must receive His favors with humility and a deep sense of gratitude; we must put into practice the lights and the instructions which we have received, and we must always be obedient to the legitimate successors of the apostles, who are the dispensers of the food of life.

Q. What are we to learn from the multitude in this day's Gospel?

A. This multitude remained with Christ for three days, and, although they were hungry and had nothing to relieve their hunger, still they cared not for their body, preferring the welfare of their soul to the most urgent wants of the body. From this we learn to esteem and value highly the word of God, to be anxious to hear the same, and to suffer courageously every bodily inconvenience when there is question of the welfare of our soul.

Q. What are we to learn from Jesus Christ?

A. We are to learn to have compassion for our brethren who are in want, and, as He used the bread reserved for Himself and for the apostles to feed the people, so also must we take pleasure in depriving ourselves of something in order to help the poor.

SEVENTH SUNDAY AFTER PENTECOST.

Gospel: St. Matthew vii. 15–21.

AT that time, Jesus said to His disciples: "Beware of false prophets, who come to you in the clothing of sheep, but inwardly they are ravening wolves. By their fruits you shall know them. Do men gather grapes of thorns, or figs of thistles? Even so every good tree bringeth forth good fruit, and the evil tree bringeth forth evil fruit. A good tree cannot bring forth evil fruit, neither can an evil tree bring forth good fruit. Every tree that bringeth not forth good fruit shall be cut down and shall be cast into the fire. Wherefore by their fruits you shall know them. Not every one that saith to Me, Lord, Lord, shall enter into the kingdom of heaven: but he that doth the will of My Father Who is in heaven, he shall enter into the kingdom of heaven."

Q. Who were called prophets in the Scriptures?

A. The word prophet means a person who, being inspired by God, announces future events and foretells what will take place in the remotest times in regard to the people and religion by the immutable will of the Lord. But the name of prophet was also given to all those good and holy men who, in the name of God, taught religion to the people; who corrected, advised, and consoled them unto eternal life, as circumstances required.

Q. Of whom, then, did Christ speak in this day's Gospel?

A. As we can call a true prophet a good and learned man who, animated by holy zeal, instructs the people in their religion, corrects their faults, consoles them in affliction, so we must call him a false prophet who, moved by passion, self-interest, and corruption of heart, misleads his neighbor by doctrines contrary to faith and good morals. From this we understand that when Jesus tells us to beware of false prophets He exhorts us to beware of those false teachers who spread error and immorality by the false doctrine coming from pride of mind and from a corrupt heart. Such false prophets among the Jews were the scribes and the doctors of the law, who endeavored to keep them away from Christ. False prophets in regard to us are all those who, under appearance of zeal for religion and love for the truth, strive to spread doctrines which do not harmonize with the spirit of the gospel.

Q. Why did Christ say that the false prophets presented themselves in the clothing of sheep, whereas they are wolves?

A. Consider the scribes and doctors of the law who lived at the time of Christ. They were very rigorous in the exterior observance of the law; they appeared to be devoured by holy zeal in all things, and they were admired by the people as models of sanctity—here they are lambs. But they were, in fact, filled with envy and hatred; they were avaricious, vindictive, covetous, hypocritical, and they sent Christ to the cross—here they are rapacious wolves. Such, also, have always been the heretics, innovators, and teachers of iniquity. Their words appear to breathe the pure love of truth, a desire to help their neighbor, and an ardent zeal for man's welfare by wishing to enlighten his mind and to reform his heart, and on this account they appear as lambs. But if you examine their manner of living and the object of their doctrine you will find that they are moved by a spirit of hatred, of pride, of sensuality, of avarice, and by a mania to draw you from God and thus cause your eternal ruin—here they appear as wolves panting for their prey.

Q. Why did Christ say that we would know the false prophets by their works?

A. As plants are known by their fruit, so also are false prophets known by their works. Thorns will not bring forth grapes, nor can you gather figs from thistles. In the same manner a corrupt heart cannot produce good actions; and if a hypocrite does something now and then that is good in itself, you will in a short time discover the motive of his actions. A corrupt heart will strive to conceal itself, but its hypocrisy is revealed by its actions. The style of dress, conversation, recreations, amusements, friendships, etc., plainly show the true condition of the heart.

Q. How can we say this?

A. We say it upon the authority of Christ. A good tree cannot bring forth bad fruit, and a bad tree cannot bring forth good fruit. The same is the case with the heart of man. An humble, patient, modest, and devout person, a person fearing God, will, as a rule, not commit sins against those beautiful virtues, unless suddenly surprised by human frailty. But a proud, dissolute, and avaricious person will fall at the slightest occasion and show his true self, no matter how hard he tries to conceal it.

Q. What did Christ want to teach us by saying that

every tree that brings not forth good fruit shall be cut down?

A. He wished to teach us that it is not enough to abstain from doing evil. God expects that when we avoid evil we should also practise the Christian virtues according to our state of life, and correspond faithfully with the graces we have received. Call to mind the servant who was punished because he did not trade with the talent he had received, and the tree that was ordered to be cut down because it brought forth no fruit, though covered with rich foliage. Woe to us if we are good Christians only in appearance, and do not bring forth the fruit of good actions!

Q. What is the last remark to be made on this Gospel?

A. We must observe what Jesus Christ says, that not every man who says to Him, Lord, Lord, will enter into the kingdom of heaven, but only those who do the will of His Eternal Father. Many Christians flatter themselves that they please God, because they daily say a certain number of prayers, assist at the holy sacrifice of the mass, and are always present at the benediction of the Blessed Sacrament; but they should reflect that all this is of no account if they do not faithfully observe the holy law of God. True devotion consists in the perfect denial of ourselves and in conforming ourselves in all things to the will of God. He who observes in all things the law of the gospel will enter into paradise, but he who makes devotion consist in words only will be excluded by Christ from the number of the elect.

EIGHTH SUNDAY AFTER PENTECOST.

Gospel: St. Luke xvi. 1–9.

AT that time, Jesus spoke to His disciples this parable: "There was a certain rich man who had a steward: and the same was accused unto him, that he had wasted his goods. And he called him, and said to him: How is it that I hear this of thee? give an account of thy stewardship, for now thou canst be steward no longer. And the steward said within himself: What shall I do, because my lord taketh away from me the stewardship? To dig I am not able; to beg I am ashamed. I know what I will do, that when I shall be removed from the stewardship they may receive me into their houses. Therefore, calling together every one of his lord's debtors, he said to the first: How much dost thou owe my lord? But he said: An hundred barrels of oil. And he said to him: Take thy bill and sit down quickly, and write fifty. Then he said to another: And how much dost thou owe? Who said: An hundred quarters of wheat. He said to him: Take thy bill, and write eighty. And the lord commended the unjust steward, forasmuch as he had done wisely: for the children of this world are wiser in their generation than the children of light. And I say to you: Make unto you friends of the mammon of iniquity: that when you shall fail they may receive you into everlasting dwellings."

Q. Why did Christ speak this parable?

A. With this parable Christ intended to rebuke the avarice of the Pharisees, who made bad use of their worldly goods; and besides, He advises us to make good use of riches, especially when they have been acquired by violating in some manner the law of God and by offending the Divine Majesty.

Q. Of whom is the steward of this parable a figure?

A. This man, as you see, had the management of a large estate, and as this was not his, but his master's property, he had no right whatever to do with it as he pleased, to neglect or squander it, and for this reason was he accused of being an unfaithful servant and was dismissed. Now this steward is a figure of ourselves, who are the administrators of the treasures which God, the Author of all good, has confided to our care. Life, health, talent, beauty, nobility, riches, all that we have, are so many trusts that God has placed in our hands, which we are to manage for our benefit, but only in the manner prescribed by Him, and not otherwise. Whenever, therefore, we make a different use of them, we are guilty before God of maladministration and of unfaithfulness, like the servant in the Gospel. Alas! What use have we so far made of so many good things which we have received from God? What have we done with our worldly goods, with our health, with our senses?

Q. What does the master's treatment of the unfaithful servant signify?

A. The master, having learned of the steward's unfaithfulness, immediately demands of him an account of his stewardship, and gives him notice that he is dismissed from office. This means that God will also one day call upon us to render an account to Him of the use we have made of His gifts, temporal and spiritual, and from that moment we can no longer have any use of them, because God will then sit in judgment upon us; this judgment takes place immediately after our death. What a terrible moment that will be for many unhappy Christians!

Q. Are the words of the steward applicable to us?

A. Certainly. He knew that he could not continue in office; he thought his situation over, and came to the conclusion that he was unable to do hard manual work, and that he was ashamed to beg. Now we should reflect thus: When we are dying we can work no more, we cannot then make good the abuse of the heavenly gifts by making a good use of them; we can no longer work by doing penance, by invoking the help of a merciful God, or the protection of the saints, because then the days of mercy and of the protection of the saints are over, and the days of rigorous justice and eternal punishment commence.

Q. What are we to think of the steward's expedient to provide for himself?

A. It was wicked, and if his master praised him, it was not on account of his stealing, but on account of the prudence and sagacity he displayed in providing for the future by making friends for himself who would assist him in want after he had lost his employment. Let us also learn to think seriously of the future, and to prevent misfortunes to our souls.

Q. What conclusion did the Divine Master draw from this?

A. He said: "Make unto you friends of the mammon of iniquity, that when you shall fail they may receive you into everlasting dwellings." By these words He counsels us, or, rather, He commands us, to think betimes of our future wants, and to make friends for ourselves in heaven, by making good use of the worldly goods we possess; that is, by doing works of mercy. Reflect that worldly possessions are sometimes acquired by unjust means; for instance, by fraud, by theft, by usury; and sometimes our ancestors, parents, or we ourselves have gained them by too much greed or anxiety, which is contrary to that detachment from worldly things which a Christian should cherish. Hence in either case they deserve to be called the fruits of iniquity. Now Christ speaks here of the latter kind, and as restitution must be made of the former, which have been acquired by fraud, theft, and usury, so also does He advise us to use that which has been amassed by sinful anxiety in doing works of mercy, in helping the poor, in offering sacrifice for the dead, in honoring the saints, so that like powerful and influential friends they may interest themselves in our behalf before God, obtain for us the divine assistance during life, pardon in death, and joy in heaven.

NINTH SUNDAY AFTER PENTECOST.

Gospel: St. Luke xix. 41–47.

AT that time: "When Jesus drew near, seeing the city, He wept over it, saying: If thou also hadst known, and that in this thy day, the things that are to thy peace; but now they are hidden from thy eyes. For the day shall come upon thee, and thy enemies shall cast a trench about thee, and compass thee round, and straighten thee on every side, and beat thee flat to the ground, and thy children who are in thee: and they shall not leave in thee a stone upon a stone, because thou hast not known the time of thy visitation. And entering into the temple,

He began to cast out them that sold therein, and them that bought, saying to them: It is written: 'My house is the house of prayer;' but you have made it a den of thieves. And He was teaching daily in the temple."

Q. Why did Jesus weep on seeing Jerusalem?

A. Tears are generally considered as a sign of weakness, but sometimes they are certainly a token of great love. The latter was the case with Jesus Christ. At beholding that unfortunate city He thought of her blindness, obstinacy, and ingratitude for the many favors which God had bestowed on her. He thought of the anger of God which she had provoked, and of the afflictions that would one day befall her on account of her crimes, and, moved by His tender charity, He shed tears over her unhappy fate.

Q. Were the predictions of Jesus in regard to Jerusalem verified?

A. Read history. Forty years after the death of the Redeemer that city was surrounded on every side by the army of Titus, shut off from all communication by three impassable barriers, divided by factions, oppressed by pestilence, hunger, and thirst, and crushed by unheard-of horrors and misery. People seeking safety by flight jumped from the walls and were killed by the fall or put to death by the Roman soldiers. Bloody contests between the factions frequently took place in the public squares and streets. Human bodies were decaying, old people were dying of hunger, and mothers in despair ate the flesh of their own children whom they had killed. In the heavens phantom armies were seen waging war, and in the temple the voices of angels were heard crying: "Let us depart hence, let us depart." The Roman soldiers finally entered the city with the sword in one hand and the torch in the other. They deluged the streets with blood, they set the houses, fortifications, and temple on fire, the whole city was reduced to ashes, a stone remained not on a stone, as had been foretold. Was not the awful prediction of Christ fulfilled?

Q. Of whom was Jerusalem a figure?

A. Jerusalem was a figure of the hardened sinner who does not profit by the grace of God, by remorse of conscience, by the counsels of his friends, or by the exhortations of the ministers of the Church. In remaining obstinate and in resisting the call of divine mercy the sinner exposes himself to the danger of being finally abandoned by God, and of becoming a victim of that unspeakable misery and horror which generally accompany final impenitence.

Q. How do we see, in the destruction of Jerusalem, the fate of the hardened sinner?

A. When an obstinate sinner is abandoned by God, bad habits, the occasions of sin, and human respect so control him that he is almost forced to commit sin, and is unable to amend his life. A perfect chaos reigns in his heart; he wishes to be in peace with God, but he also wants to sin. He would like to enjoy peace of heart, but he also wants to gratify his passions. He fails in good works, is deprived of spiritual help, and carried away by corruption; he cares no longer for friends, parents, family, or for himself. The thought of the punishment due his iniquities causes him to despair. He dies and, from temporal, he passes to eternal sufferings.

Q. What are we to conclude from this?

A. It is the greatest misfortune to close our ears to

the voice of God when He comes to visit us with His grace. We should, therefore, profit by the call and invitation of the Lord while we have time, so that He may not abandon us as He did ungrateful Jerusalem.

Q. What else is related in the Gospel of to-day?

A. It is related that Jesus Christ cast out of the temple those who were carrying on a profane traffic. From this we are to learn that we provoke Christ when we seek in the house of the Lord anything but God. If we go to church out of habit or curiosity, or to pass the time; if we are distracted, undevout, irreverent; if we go to see or be seen; if, in a word, we act like sinners in the house of prayer, we deserve to be driven out, and we deserve to feel the weight of God's anger, for He is jealous of His house, where He expects our adoration and dispenses His mercies.

TENTH SUNDAY AFTER PENTECOST.

Gospel: St. Luke xviii. 9–14.

AT that time: "To some who trusted in themselves as just and despised others Jesus spoke this parable: Two men went up into the temple to pray: the one a Pharisee and the other a publican. The Pharisee standing prayed thus with himself: O God! I give Thee thanks that I am not as the rest of men: extortioners, unjust, adulterers, as also is this publican. I fast twice in a week; I give tithes of all that I possess. And the publican, standing afar off, would not so much as lift up his eyes toward heaven, but struck his breast, saying: O God! be merciful to me a sinner! I say to you this man went down into his house justified rather than the other;

because every one that exalteth himself shall be humbled: and he that humbleth himself shall be exalted."

Q. Why did Jesus Christ speak this parable?

A. By this parable the Divine Saviour wanted to teach those who were present, as well as all future Christians, how necessary it is to close our eyes to our own merits and virtues in order to avoid the sin of pride. He assures us that only the humble of heart are pleasing to God, and they alone obtain His favors.

Q. Of whom was the Pharisee a figure?

A. The Pharisee was a true image of a man full of himself and carried away by pride. He boasted that he was not like other people; that he had no faults, that he had no vices, that he was not an adulterer, but that he practised virtue and was faithful in the observance of the law. But, while he praised himself, he uncharitably condemned the publican. Such is the proud man. He alone is learned, prudent, and skilful; he alone is the model according to which all should shape their actions; he alone is deserving of esteem, honors, and preferment. If others do not praise him, he will do it himself; and when he aspires to an office of honor or to some distinction, he does not scruple to calumniate others, to be cruel and to deceive; he sacrifices all to his passions, which he will gratify at any cost. This man in his pride would have sacrificed the whole Jewish nation if he could have done so.

Q. What are we to learn from this?

A. We should learn to avoid the vice of pride and not to confide in our own good qualities, if we happen to have any, in order not to become, like the

Pharisee, an object of aversion to God. To avoid this vice, let us bear in mind that the proud man is odious to heaven and earth, and that God, as St. Peter says, resists the proud and covers them with confusion, as he did Lucifer, the sons of Babel, Holofernes, and many others.

Q. But what are we to do when we know that we have good qualities?

A. We should then remember that those good qualities do not belong to us, but that they are gifts of the mercy and grace of that God Who, in a moment, can deprive us of them on account of our pride and of His justice. On the other hand, who is certain whether he deserves love or hatred, notwithstanding the good testimony of his conscience? Urias thought he was a favorite of his sovereign; and, full of this confidence, he carried in his own hand the irrevocable decree of his death. The Bishops of Ephesus, Pergamus, Sardis, and Laodicea believed they were near God, whilst God Himself complained of them to St. John, the apostle. We should not be too confident in glorifying our own good qualities. In the eyes of God even the stars of heaven are not pure.

Q. Of whom is the publican a figure?

A. He is a figure of the sinner who, by the grace of God, knows his failings, humbles himself, and asks for mercy. He would not even lift his eyes to heaven, and God looked down on him with the eyes of a father. He asks for mercy, and God, besides forgiving him his sins, bestows on him His benediction and graces. Let us learn from this publican; let us not hide our sins, but acknowledge them; let us prostrate ourselves before God and confess that we are unworthy of His favors, but let us always hope to obtain them of His infinite goodness through the merits of Jesus Christ, remembering what St. Peter said, that God gives His grace to the humble.

Q. What will help us to be humble?

A. We should consider what we were, what we are, and what we shall be, both in regard to soul and body. In regard to the body we were once nothing; now we are a clod of earth, subject to many miseries, and one day we shall be a heap of bones and ashes. In regard to the soul we were once slaves of the devil, vessels of wrath deserving hell, now we are in need of everything; we are poor sinners exposed to all kinds of dangers, and one day God will judge whether we shall be rewarded with the saints in heaven or punished with the reprobates in hell.

ELEVENTH SUNDAY AFTER PENTECOST.

Gospel: St. Mark vii. 31–37.

AT that time: "Jesus going out of the coasts of Tyre, He came by Sidon to the Sea of Galilee through the midst of the coasts of Decapolis. And they bring to Him one deaf and dumb; and they besought Him that He would lay His hand upon him. And taking him from the multitude apart, He put His fingers into his ears, and spitting, He touched his tongue. And looking up to heaven, He groaned, and said to him: Ephpheta, which is, Be thou opened. And immediately his ears were opened, and the string of his tongue was loosed, and he spoke right. And He charged them that they should tell no man. But the more He charged them so much the more a great deal did they publish it. And so much the more did they wonder, saying: He hath done all things well: He hath made both the deaf to hear and the dumb to speak."

Q. Of whom was the deaf and dumb man a figure?

A. He was a figure of the human race, which by the sin of Adam was rendered unable to hear the voice of salvation and to pronounce the words that would redound to the glory of God and to the good of their souls.

Q. Why did Christ take him apart from the multitude?

A. From this we should learn that in order to cure men of the infirmity of sin it is necessary to free them from the superstition, the corruption, and the false maxims of the world, and to teach them to follow doctrines and laws different from those of the Gentiles.

Q. Why did Christ put His finger into the ears, and with His own spittle touch the tongue of the deaf and dumb man?

A. His finger signifies the divine Omnipotence, and the spittle the divine Wisdom. By so doing Christ gave us to understand that in order to open the ears and to loosen the tongue of our soul the work of the Holy Ghost, Who is the finger of the Eternal Father, is absolutely necessary; but that the Holy Ghost would not have done this work, if the Eternal Wisdom, made man, had not merited it for us by His passion and death.

Q. Why did Jesus, before curing him, raise His eyes to heaven and groan?

A. By groaning Jesus gave us to understand how deplorable the condition of mankind is, which through its own fault has become deaf and dumb in regard to God, and how great is His compassion for mankind. By looking up to heaven He asked the mercy and power of the Eternal Father to cure the afflicted man.

Q. How are the words, "He spoke right," verified in the human race?

A. Consider how a Christian, by virtue of baptism, has his ears opened to the voice of Heaven, and how he speaks of God, and you will see the prodigy realized. If we hear the voice that invites us to do good and abstain from evil; if we hear the voice that reproaches us for our faults and encourages us in the exercise of virtues; if we confess our weakness and praise God, all this is a prodigy of that finger of grace which opened our ears and loosened our tongue to hear the truth and to speak words of salvation for ourselves, and words of glory for the author of our regeneration.

Q. Can we say that a Christian is sometimes deaf and dumb?

A. He is certainly so if he is hardened in sin. He then does not acknowledge his guilt, he does not pray to God or praise Him, and while he talks too much of the things of the world he is mute about the things of God. Besides, by remaining obstinate in his sins he does not hear the voice of grace, the internal inspirations, the invitations of the divine mercy; and like a deaf man who does not profit by the words spoken to him, even for his own good, he draws no profit from counsel, advice, or correction.

Q. Why did Jesus forbid the people to make this miracle known?

A. To teach us not to seek human praise and reward when we have done a good work. By putting to good use the natural or supernatural gifts we have received from God, we surely can do great things for the glory of God, for the good of society, and for our neighbor's welfare; but, content with having done our duty, we must not publish our merit to the world, we must not wish for human reward, we must avoid all praise and say to ourselves, as Jesus commands us, that we are useless servants on earth.

Q. Why did the multitude not obey the command of Jesus?

A. Here is another wholesome lesson for us. Let us do all the good we can, and let us evade the applause of men and await our reward from God. After the example of the multitude we are not bound to keep silence when our benefactors are concerned, should their modesty even command us to do so. Let us praise their virtue, let us show our gratitude and publish their good works, when it will serve as a good example to society, and when it is for the greater glory of the Lord.

Q. What are we to learn from all this?

A. As this deaf and dumb man was a figure of the human race, we are to learn how sad our condition has been through the fault of our first parents, and we are to cherish sentiments of lively gratitude to Jesus Christ, Who by His all-powerful grace has delivered us from it. As this man is, in a more particular sense, a figure of the hardened sinner who hears not the voice of God and has no tongue to confess his guilt or to praise the Divine Majesty, we are to learn to avoid such a deplorable state of obstinate impenitence, and, after the example of the kind-hearted multitude, we should beseech Jesus to lay the hand of His grace on our deaf and dumb brethren and grant them that which is unto life eternal.

TWELFTH SUNDAY AFTER PENTECOST.

Gospel: St. Luke x. 23–37.

AT that time, Jesus said to His disciples: "Blessed are the eyes that see the things which you see. For I say to you that many prophets and kings have desired to see the things that you see, and have not seen them, and to hear the things that you hear, and have not heard them. And behold a certain lawyer stood up, tempting Him, and saying: Master, what must I do to possess eternal life? But He said to him: What is written in the law? how readest thou? He answering, said: Thou shalt love the Lord thy God with thy whole heart, and with thy whole soul, and with all thy strength, and with all thy mind, and thy neighbor as thyself. And He said to him: Thou hast answered right: this do, and thou shalt live. But he, willing to justify himself, said to Jesus: And who is my neighbor? And Jesus answering, said: A certain man went down from Jerusalem to Jericho and fell among robbers, who also stripped him, and, having wounded him, went away, leaving him half dead. And it chanced that a certain priest went down the same way, and seeing him, passed by. In like manner also a Levite, when he was near the place and saw him, passed by. But a certain Samaritan, being on his journey, came near him, and seeing him, was moved with compassion;

and going up to him, bound up his wounds, pouring in oil and wine, and setting him upon his own beast, brought him to an inn, and took care of him. And the next day he took out two pence, and gave to the host, and said: Take care of him; and whatsoever thou shalt spend over and above, I at my return will repay thee. Which of these three in thy opinion was neighbor to him that fell among the robbers? But he said: He that showed mercy to him. And Jesus said to him: Go and do thou in like manner."

Q. What did the apostles see in Christ?

A. The apostles saw in Jesus Christ the Eternal Word, the only begotten Son of the living God, the Messias promised to the patriarchs, foretold by the prophets, and expected of nations, while ignorant and carnal men saw in Him only the son of a carpenter, an obscure and poor man of Nazareth, a son of Adam like all the rest of men.

Q. What did the apostles hear from Jesus Christ?

A. They heard truths until then unknown, and words of eternal life not understood and not believed by the greater majority of those who followed the Divine Master, without understanding the meaning of His parables and the eloquence of His miracles.

Q. Who were those who desired to see and hear what the apostles saw and heard, but could not?

A. They were all those who lived and died before Christ, who, believing and hoping in the future Messias, desired to see Him and His miracles which had been foretold and hear His heavenly doctrine. But they were prevented by death from enjoying the longed-for consolation.

Q. Were the apostles the only fortunate ones?

A. No. All Christians, and especially we who live among so many that have fallen into schism and heresy. In the Man of Nazareth, that is, in Jesus Christ, we see with the eyes of faith the Saviour. In His miracles we see the divinity of His doctrine confirmed. In His manner of living we see the model we are to imitate. His words are not obscure to us as they were to many; we understand them as the apostles did, because from them and from their legitimate successors we have been taught beyond any doubt their true and sublime sense.

Q. What do you think of that doctor of the law who tempted Jesus by putting a question to Him?

A. We should detest his duplicity, and admire the prudent answer of Jesus Christ, an answer that may be applied to many Christians who, wanting to live according to their own fancy, invent new doctrines and capricious rules, when the gospel has already laid down the law in regard to our gains, our amusements, our food, our clothing—in fact, in regard to all the works of a Christian.

Q. Of whom was the man who fell among robbers a figure?

A. He was an image of the human race, which by disobedience fell from the state of grace into a state of sin. Jerusalem, the city of the Lord, built upon a mountain, represents the state of grace, and Jericho, a city built in a valley, represents the state of sin. The human race fell under the power of the infernal robber, who, having despoiled it of original innocence and grace, wounded it in the intellect, the heart, and the will, and left it on the road to perdition, prostrate in its misfortune and incapable by its natural strength to rise again.

Q. What does it mean that the man was wounded and not dead?

A. It means that the human race was not lost beyond redemption like the bad angels who, having once sinned, were condemned to eternal woe, but that although its wounds were mortal, it could still be cured. This cure, however, could not be effected by all the just, nor by the patriarchs and prophets, who until Christ's time had lived upon the earth, and of whom the priest was the figure, nor by the precepts, ceremonies, and legal sacrifices, of which the Levite was a figure, but only by the Samaritan, that is, the Eternal Word, a stranger to us, because He is God and the only faithful guardian of our soul, because, loving us from all eternity, He watched over our welfare.

Q. Whom did the Samaritan represent?

A. He represented Jesus Christ, and mark well the circumstances. The Samaritan was passing by the place where the wounded man lay, he sees him, he is moved to compassion, and he approaches him to treat his wounds and to help him in any other way. It was the same with Christ; He was the true Samaritan, the eternal Guardian, the Saviour of men, a stranger to us before His incarnation, like unto us with the exception of sin, and separated from sinners. He became a pilgrim and dwelt among us by becoming man, He looked with compassion on the human race, prostrate on the earth and covered with wounds, and He undertook the great task of healing and restoring it to life.

Q. What did He do to heal the human race?

A. This divine Samaritan, in order to heal our wounds, approached us by assuming our nature. He treated our spiritual wounds with the oil of grace and with the wine of heavenly charity. He bound up these wounds with the bandages of His holy law, and He brought us to the inn of salvation, suffering in His humanity the punishment due to the sinner, and bringing us back, by His passion and death, to the bosom of the Holy Church, where we are under the protection of His ministers, whose office it is to heal our infirmities and prepare us for life eternal.

Q. What do the two pence signify which the Samaritan gave to the host to take care of the wounded man?

A. We have received a remedy for the wounds inflicted by the devil in the passion and in the grace of Jesus Christ. These wounds might grow worse and be once more the cause of our death But our divine Guardian, after having given us in charge of His ministers, the priests, has given to them two most efficient means to provide for our wants. These means are instruction and the sacraments. By the first we are enabled to know what we should believe and what we should do. By the second we are enabled to regain grace if we have lost it, or to increase it if we already possess it.

Q. What is the meaning of these words: "Whatsoever thou shalt spend over and above, I at my return will repay thee"?

A. Jesus Christ, having completed the work of redemption, left this world, ascended into heaven, and will return at the end of the world. In the meantime, we are confided to the care of the priests, His ministers, and they in His name must provide for our eternal welfare. But if they, in the discharge of their duties, do more than what they are strictly bound to do, they will receive an especial reward from Christ on the day of judgment, when He will reurn to this world to punish the wicked and to reward the good for all they have done, the former against Him, and the latter for His glory.

Q. Is this promise of Christ only for His priests?

A. This promise was made to them in a special manner, but it was also addressed to all who do more for their neighbors' welfare than they are in duty bound to do. A parent, a teacher, an employer, a superior, a sovereign, who is not content with simply doing his duty toward those confided to his care, but who with an extraordinary zeal endeavors to promote their spiritual welfare and their progress in Christian virtue and perfection, will undoubtedly receive a special reward from Jesus Christ, and will one day enjoy a greater glory in heaven.

THIRTEENTH SUNDAY AFTER PENTECOST.

Gospel: St. Luke xvii. 11–19.

AT that time, "As Jesus was going to Jerusalem, He passed through the midst of Samaria and Galilee. And as He entered into a certain town there met Him ten men that were lepers, who stood afar off and lifted up their voice, saying: Jesus, Master, have mercy on us. Whom when He saw, He said. Go, show yourselves to the priests. And it came to pass, as they went, they were made clean. And one of them, when he saw that he was made clean, went back, with a loud voice glorifying God, and he fell on his face, before His feet, giving thanks: and this was a Samaritan. And Jesus answering, said: Were not ten made clean? and where are the nine? There is no one found to return and give glory to God, but this stranger. And He said to him: Arise, go thy way, for thy faith hath made thee whole."

Q. Of whom were these lepers a figure?

A. St. Augustine says they were an image of heretics and also of sinners, and especially of those afflicted with the vice of impurity.

Q. Why were they in a special manner a figure of the impure sinner?

A. As a leper is a disgusting object to men, so is a lewd sinner an abominable object to the eyes of God. As lepers were to be avoided because of the danger of contracting their contagious disease, so also must lewd persons be avoided, because they easily communicate to others their spiritual disease.

Q. Why did He send them to the priests?

A. It was prescribed in Leviticus (xiii.) that lepers when cured of their disease should present themselves to the priest to be declared cured, after which they were restored to the society of their fellow-men and introduced into the temple. On this account Jesus sent those men to the priests that they might be witnesses of their cure, and do what was commanded by the law in such cases.

Q. How in this were they like the lewd sinner?

A. According to the Old Law it was necessary for lepers to have recourse to the priest to be cleansed from the legal impurity and restored to society. In like manner those who are infected by the vice of impurity have need of the ministry of the confessor to be prepared to participate in the sacraments, to be helped to overcome their bad habits, and to persevere in their good resolutions. For such, frequent confession is undoubtedly the most efficacious means of reform.

Q. What does it mean that as they went they were made clean?

A. Their cure did not depend on the work of the priests, but on the grace of Jesus Christ, and as they believed in Him and hastened to see the priests as He had commanded them, as they went the wish of their hearts was granted, and they were cured as a reward of their faith and obedience.

Q. What meaning has all this for us?

A. It means that our deliverance from the leprosy of sin does not depend on the words of the priest, who judges by the exterior, but is effected by the power of Christ, Who sees our interior. Hence the absolution of the priest is of no advantage to us if he was too easy in giving it or if we obtained it by fraud. The absolution is of no avail if God, Who searches the heart, does not confirm it. It also means that the operation of grace in our souls and the abundance of the divine mercy will be in proportion to our faith and to our prompt obedience to the voice of God.

Q. What are we to learn from the Samaritan who returned to thank Jesus?

A. We are to learn to be really grateful to the divine mercy by which, through the merits of Jesus Christ, we have been cleansed not only once, but very often from the leprosy of sin. Let us not content ourselves w th mere words, but as this Samaritan glorified God with loud voice and, prostrate at the feet of the divine Master, adored Him, so should we by our actions and good example proclaim the power of His grace, and make known to all our faith and our submission to the majesty of the Lord.

Q. What are we to learn from the nine ungrateful ones?

A. Inasmuch as we are indignant at their ingratitude, we should learn how disgraceful and infamous our conduct would be if we were insensible or ungrateful for benefits which we have received either from God or from man.

FOURTEENTH SUNDAY AFTER PENTECOST.

Gospel: St. Matthew vi. 24-33.

AT that time, Jesus said to His disciples: "No man can serve two masters. For either he will hate the one and love the other, or he will sustain the one and despise the other. You cannot serve God and mammon. Therefore I say to you be not solicitous for your life, what you shall eat, nor for your body, what you shall put on. Is not the life more than the meat, and the body more than the raiment? Behold the birds of the air, for they neither sow, nor do they reap, nor gather into barns: and your Heavenly Father feedeth them. Are not you of much more value than they? And which of you by taking thought can add to his stature one cubit? And for raiment why are you solicitous? Consider the lilies of the field, how they grow: they labor not, neither do they spin. But I say to you that not even Solomon in all his glory was arrayed as one of these. And if the grass of the field, which is to-day, and to-morrow is cast into the oven, God doth so clothe, how much more you, O ye of little faith? Be not solicitous therefore, saying: What shall we eat, or what shall we drink, or wherewith shall we be clothed? For after all these things do the heathens seek. For your Father knoweth that you have need of all these things Seek ye therefore first the kingdom of God and His justice, and all these things shall be added unto you."

Q. What was the object of these words of Christ?

A. The object was to reprove the extreme anxiety and attachment for the riches of this world, and besides to exhort us to place our trust in divine Providence.

Q. What did Christ say to detach us from the love of riches?

A. He said that if the love for them is bad, it will surely rule our heart, and when this is the case, it will be impossible for us to please God, as it is utterly impossible to please two masters at one and the same time who are so opposed to each other in all things as are the love of riches and the love of God.

Q. Why are the love of God and the love of riches entirely opposed to each other?

A. It would be too much to say all that proves this, hence let it suffice to say that the love of God is always and only occupied with the things of heaven, that it despises the things of the world, and voluntarily distributes them to the poor; that the love of riches, on the contrary, is only eager to obtain the things of the world, is never satisfied with its profits, and instead of helping the poor and needy it rather endeavors to rob them and to grow richer by their blood.

Q. What does He say to encourage us to trust in divine Providence?

A. In order to encourage us to place our confidence in God, Jesus Christ commands us not to be solicitous about what we are to eat, or wherewith we are to clothe ourselves, because that God Who in His goodness has made us out of nothing cannot and will not refuse us what is necessary for our sustenance, if with childlike confidence we have recourse to His fatherly love.

Q. How is all this proved?

A. It is proved by what happens every day. We see the birds of the air are fed, and the flowers of the field are clad in beautiful clothing. Now if God in His providence preserves that order of things by which the birds receive their food and the flowers their beautiful vesture, how much more will He provide the necessaries of life for us, He being our Father. Hence the Holy Ghost said by the mouth of David: "*Jacta super Dominum curam tuam, et ipse te enutriet.*"

Q. If this be the case, is it not useless to work all day? Is it not enough to have confidence in God?

A. Bear in mind that Christ forbids us to be overanxious or uneasy, but He does not dispense us from using our strength. He who would lead an idle and careless life would be unworthy of God's bounty and would insult divine Providence. We must earn our bread in the sweat of our brow, but our efforts will be fruitless if they have not the blessing of God. If we cannot do anything for ourselves, the powerful hand of God will help us, when like good children we have recourse to His paternal love.

Q. Can you give some examples of this divine Providence?

A. We find many examples in the Holy Scriptures, and leaving aside Agar, who was provided with water for her dying son Ismael, Susanna, who was provided with a protector who defended her innocence and delivered her from death, Daniel, who was provided with food in the lions' den and was saved from death, it will suffice to remember the Hebrew people when they were in the desert. They had no bread, and God sent them quails, and daily gave them manna for forty years. They frequently had no water to drink, and God miraculously turned the bitter waters to sweet, and gave them water out of a rock. They could procure no garments, and God preserved for forty years the clothes they brought with them from Egypt. Now this divine Providence that cared for the Hebrews in the desert will also take care of us. We often enjoy the benefits of this divine Providence without knowing it, but the Holy Ghost assures us that the just man has never been forsaken, and God as a loving Father always watches over us.

Q. What are we to do to deserve such a Providence?

A. Jesus Christ Himself has taught us, and especially in this day's Gospel He tells what we must do, when He says: "Seek first the kingdom of God and His justice."

Q. What did He mean by this?

A. He wished to teach us that our only desire and

our constant prayer should be that God may be glorified, and that we may obtain the necessary means to gain heaven, that is, an abundance of grace, holiness of life, the possession of virtue, and perseverance in good. When, therefore, the kingdom of God is our only object, when we are faithful, just, and persevering in the divine service, then divine Providence will provide us with the necessary temporal things, without our being anxious about them, in the same manner as the earth brought forth its fruit without being cultivated when Adam was in the state of original innocence.

FIFTEENTH SUNDAY AFTER PENTECOST.

Gospel: St. Luke vii. 11–16.

AT that time: "Jesus went into a city that is called Naim, and there went with Him His disciples and a great multitude. And when He came nigh to the gate of the city, behold a dead man was carried out, the only son of his mother: and she was a widow: and a great multitude of the city was with her. Whom when the Lord had seen, being moved with mercy toward her, He said to her: Weep not. And He came near and touched the bier. (And they that carried it stood still.) And He said: Young man, I say to thee, arise. And he that was dead sat up and began to speak. And He gave him to his mother. And there came a fear on them all, and they glorified God, saying: A great prophet is risen up among us, and God hath visited His people."

Q. Was this meeting of Jesus with the funeral a mere accident?

A. According to the history of this fact it would

seem to have been simply an accident, but the sacred interpreters say that Jesus went purposely to Naim and arranged all in such a manner that He was at the gate of the city at the proper time, in order to work the astonishing miracle, which inspired with faith those who beheld it, and which teaches us a lesson of the greatest importance.

Q. Of whom was that dead man a figure?
A. He was the image of a sinner dead in the eyes of God, more disfigured by his sins than a corpse, deprived of every spiritual good and of the strength to do works for life eternal.

Q. Of whom was the sorrowful mother who followed the bier a figure?
A. She was a figure of the Church, which never loses sight of those of her children whom sin has deprived of life. She continually laments their condition, desires their conversion, and prays for it fervently and constantly from the mercy of God through the merits of Jesus Christ.

Q. What are we to recognize in the bier and in the four men who carried it?
A. In the bier we are to recognize our fallen nature in which we are obliged to lie, and in the four pall-bearers the ruling vices that carry us to destruction. One who is in the state of sin, not out of human frailty, but rather out of pure malice, lies, like a corpse on the bier, on the bed of sin, and the ruling passions carry him rapidly to the grave of eternal death.

Q. What do we behold in Jesus Christ moved to compassion for this mother?

A. We see the same Jesus Christ now reigning in heaven, Who by the constant and fervent prayers of our common mother the Church is moved to compassion for poor sinners and gives them the grace to rise again from their sins, as is daily the case in the conversion of so many Christians.

Q. What is meant by Christ touching the bier, and by the bearers standing still?

A. This signifies that God, in the conversion of sinners, who are carried to perdition by their ruling passions and bad habits, touches with His grace our weak human nature in such a manner that the soul is no longer carried away by the torrent of corruption, and that, moreover, He causes the vices and ruling passions which carried it to the grave of eternal death to stand still, and not as before to reduce it to further errors by their furious attacks.

Q. Why did Christ command with such power the dead young man to arise?

A. By this our Divine Master wished to teach us that for the conversion of a sinner, who is a slave of his passions and bad habits, a powerful and special grace is necessary, which almost like a miracle stops the course of the predominant passions, and hinders them from going further. Oh, how should habitual sinners tremble, when they reflect that God gives this grace out of pure mercy, notwithstanding our unworthiness, and that He does not give it to all, but only to whom He pleases, and when and how He pleases, for no one can merit this grace.

Q. The young man sat up; what are we to learn from this?

A. When God by His grace commands a sinner to rise from his spiritual death he is aroused from his deadly lethargy, he opens his eyes to the light of faith, he speaks confessing his sins, and those very passions that formerly controlled him he now controls and subjects to the power of his will. Recall to mind St. Paul, St. Augustine, and St. Margaret, and you will see how at the command of grace they shook off the sleep of death, and how from that very moment they made use of those talents, of that ardent character, and that tendency of their hearts, which had once been the sad cause of their transgressions, as a triumph of virtue.

Q. Jesus gave the young man into the care of his mother; what does this teach us?

A. When God by His grace converts a sinner, He restores him to the Church, his mother, who gains in him a son who was dead to her, and she rejoices at his return to spiritual life. Besides, God confides this son, risen to a new life, to her maternal care that she may help him to gain strength, that she may enlighten, direct, console, encourage, and guide him on the way of penance, perseverance, and perfection.

Q. What are we to think of the multitude that was so astonished?

A. This should not surprise us; it is rather surprising that so many Christians do not take notice of a greater miracle that God continually works in a spiritual manner in the Church. Every day His powerful grace recalls from death to life many souls, and perhaps even our own: yet scarcely any one thinks of giving Him that glory and thanksgiving which are His due.

Q. What are we to learn from this Gospel?

A. Let us learn to weep with the Church over the unhappy death of so many of our brethren who are the slaves of sin, and to pray with her that the Divine Mercy may recall them to life. Let us learn to beg Jesus to come to meet us in His great charity, as He did the dead young man of Naim, when we have had the misfortune to fall into mortal sin. Lastly, let us learn to thank God for all He has done for us, either by resuscitating us when we were in the state of sin, or by preserving us from what might again cause our spiritual death.

SIXTEENTH SUNDAY AFTER PENTECOST.

Gospel: St. Luke xiv. 1-11.

AT that time: "When Jesus went into the house of one of the chief of the Pharisees, on the Sabbath-day, to eat bread, they watched Him. And behold there was a certain man before Him that had the dropsy. And Jesus answering, spoke to the lawyers and Pharisees, saying: Is it lawful to heal on the Sabbath-day? But they held their peace. But He, taking him, healed him, and sent him away. And answering them, He said: Which of you shall have an ass or an ox fall into a pit and will not immediately draw him out on the Sabbath-day? And they could not answer Him to these things. And He spoke a parable also to them that were invited, marking how they chose the first seats at the table, saying to them: When thou art invited to a wedding, sit not down in the first place, lest perhaps one more honorable than thou be invited by him: and he that invited thee and him come and say to thee: Give this man place; and then thou begin with shame to take the lowest place. But when thou art invited, go, sit down in the lowest place: that when he who invited thee cometh he may say to thee: Friend, go up higher. Then shalt thou have glory before them that sit at table with thee. Because every one that exalteth himself shall be humbled: and he that humbleth himself shall be exalted."

Q. How could Jesus accept the invitation to the table of a Pharisee?

A. It is true the Pharisees were bad men, but Jesus Christ did not refuse to enter the house of this man, who was one of the most distinguished among them, because He wished to take this opportunity to benefit them by His doctrines and miracles; thus teaching us not to repel or avoid sinners as long as there is any hope of doing them good.

Q. What miracle did Christ work, and what doctrines did He teach on this occasion?

A. The Gospel relates that on this occasion He healed a man who had the dropsy, and He taught those present as well as us also that it is not forbidden to heal the sick on the Sabbath-day. Besides, He showed that we must avoid pride and cultivate humility.

Q. Of whom was the man that had the dropsy a figure?

A. St. Augustine says that he was a figure of the rich miser who the more he has the more he wants, after the manner of dropsical patients, who the fuller they are of water the more they want to drink.

Q. Is this man a figure of anything else?

A. According to St. Augustine, the dropsy of this

man signified any other predominating passion of a sinner. Any passion, when it takes possession of the heart, becomes insatiable, and the more it is gratified the worse it becomes, like the thirst of one afflicted with dropsy. If we notice a drunkard, a proud man, a libertine, an ambitious woman, a miser, we see that the habitual debauch, the beastly excesses, the most extravagant fashions, and the greatest gain do not satisfy their desires, and, much as they may gratify their whims, they never have enough.

Q. How did Jesus prove that it was not forbidden to heal the sick on the Sabbath-day?

A. He proved it from the example of the Pharisees themselves, by saying that if they did not scruple to draw from the pit an ass or an ox that had fallen into it, because their interest required them to do so, much less should there be any difficulty in curing a sick person for charity's sake and for the glory of God. Those Pharisees were impious men, says the venerable Bede. Through avarice they would violate the law of the Sabbath, and at the same time they accused Christ of violating the Sabbath because He cured a man through charity.

Q. Were the Pharisees convinced by this reasoning?

A. As the Gospel says, they felt that they were silenced, and held their peace. Yet, instead of being enlightened, they became more obstinate in finding fault with Christ, and, as St. John relates, they persecuted Him, telling the people that He was not a friend of God, because He did not observe the Sabbath.

Q. What else worthy of remark took place on this occasion?

A. That happened which often happens in our

day. The Pharisees who had been invited were full of self-conceit. Each one of them had a high opinion of himself; each fancied that he was greater than the others, and each sought to be preferred and to have the first seat at the table.

Q. And what did Jesus Christ do then?

A. Jesus Christ, knowing the ambitious desires of their hearts, gave them the important advice to select the lowest place, so as not to expose themselves to the shame of being obliged to give up the highest place by the command of the host, who had destined it for one who was superior in merit.

Q. What did Christ mean by this counsel?

A. He wished to correct those proud men, by making them understand how improper their ambitious behavior was in selecting the best places; at the same time He taught all future Christians to close their eyes to their own merits, not to exact attentions, and to believe themselves inferior to others, by always with sincerity of heart choosing the last place for themselves.

Q. With what promise did Christ confirm this lesson?

A. He confirmed it by saying that he who exalts himself shall be humbled, and he who humbles himself shall be exalted.

Q. Before whom will the proud be humbled and the humble exalted?

A. Before God and men. Even the world despises the proud, and when it can humble them it does it with pleasure. On the other hand, it loves, esteems, and praises the truly humble, and is pleased when their merit is appreciated. God, says St. Hilary, will humble the pride of the ambitious and glorify the humble, if not in this life, certainly and forever in the next.

Q. In what does true humility consist?

A. It consists in considering ourselves as nothing before God and men, for indeed we are nothing, and all we have, in the order of nature or in the order of grace, comes from God, as also all we do, great or small, depends on His help and goodness.

Q. What are the degrees of Christian humility?

A. They are as follows: To know ourselves, our insufficiency, our natural misery, and hence to have a low opinion of ourselves. Secondly, to bear patiently and with fortitude humiliations, wherever they may come from. Finally, to rejoice in these humiliations and to say with David: It is good, O Lord, that Thou hast humbled me.

SEVENTEENTH SUNDAY AFTER PENTECOST.

Gospel: St. Matthew xxii. 35-46.

AT that time, the Pharisees came nigh to Jesus: "And one of them, a doctor of the law, asked Him, tempting Him: Master, which is the great commandment in the law? Jesus said to him: Thou shalt love the Lord thy God with thy whole heart, and with thy whole soul, and with thy whole mind. This is the greatest and the first commandment. And the second is like to this: Thou shalt love thy neighbor as thyself. On these two commandments dependeth the whole law and the prophets. And the Pharisees being gathered together, Jesus asked them, saying: What think you of Christ? Whose son is He? They say to Him: David's. He saith to them: How then doth David in spirit call Him Lord, saying: The Lord said to my Lord: Sit on My right hand until I make Thy enemies Thy footstool? If David then call Him Lord, how is He his son? And no man was able to answer Him a word; neither durst any man from that day forth ask Him any more questions."

Q. In what sense was the question of the Pharisee a temptation?

A. To understand the force and the malice of this question of the Pharisee, which the Gospel calls a temptation, it is necessary to know that in Christ's time there was a question which was the greater obligation: to love God or to offer in the temple the sacrifices commanded by the law. Many were of the opinion that the first and greatest commandment was that of offering sacrifice in the temple. On this account the doctor of the law asked Jesus Christ which was the greatest commandment of the law, with the intention to induce Him to decide the question, with the danger to Himself of displeasing one or the other party, if He did not support His assertion by undeniable proof.

Q. What was Christ's answer?

A. He answered that the first and greatest commandment was to love God above all things, with our whole heart, with our whole soul, and with all our strength.

Q. What do you think of this precept?

A. There is nothing more reasonable and just. God is perfection itself, the fountain and the source of all good; therefore He must be loved for what

He is in preference to all other things, and He must be loved with our whole heart and with our whole soul, cost us what it may. God has created us for the sole purpose that we may love Him, and hereafter enjoy Him for all eternity as a reward of this love; therefore we are bound by the law of nature to love Him. God is the absolute Lord of our life and of all we have on this earth; therefore we are bound in justice to love Him. God has bestowed on us innumerable natural and supernatural benefits, and continues to do so; therefore we are bound to love Him out of gratitude, and if man would not love Him He would be worse than the brute animals, that show themselves grateful to those who feed them.

Q. Why did Christ say that the precept to love God is the first and greatest commandment?

A. Because charity is the greatest of the virtues, the root, the support, and the crown of all the others. Without charity, all the acts of devotion are nothing; without charity, patience, generosity, meekness, chastity, and all other good qualities avail nothing; without charity, we are objects of hatred in the sight of God. Hence St. Paul says: "If I should speak with the tongues of angels, if I possessed all knowledge, if I should distribute all my goods to the poor, if I worked miracles, if I should deliver my body to be burned, and have not charity, I am nothing more than a sounding brass or a tinkling cymbal" (I. Cor. xiii.).

Q. Which is the second great commandment?

A. Christ has told us what it is. It is to love our neighbor as ourselves; that is, we must love him sincerely, ardently, and effectively, but always for the love of God.

Q. How are we to practise this love?

A. The same divine Teacher taught us the way to practise it, when He said: "Do unto others as you wish them to do unto you." Hence St. Augustine, explaining this maxim, says: "Whatever good we wish for ourselves, the same we must procure for our neighbor, and the evil that we fear we must prevent from befalling our neighbor."

Q. Does he who treats his neighbor kindly and generously, but without reference to God, fulfil the commandment?

A. God has commanded us to love our neighbor as ourselves, but always for love of Him, in regard to Him, with eyes fixed on Him alone. Therefore he who loves and gives abundantly to his neighbor through human sensibility, through natural goodness of heart, or through philanthropy, would not satisfy the precept. He would deserve the praise and the gratitude of men, but he would merit no supernatural reward.

Q. Why did Jesus say that "on these two commandments dependeth the whole law and the prophets"?

A. He said this because all the other precepts of the law and the teachings of the prophets, that is, of those who speak to us in God's name, are founded on the commandment of the love of God and of our neighbor, and all flow therefrom in such a manner that he whose heart is animated by charity observes the whole law; but when this virtue, which constitutes the essence of a Christian, is wanting, the whole law is transgressed.

Q. After Christ had taught such a wholesome

lesson, what else, according to the Gospel, did He do?

A. Wishing to render good for evil, He took the occasion to enlighten and to lead His tempters and His enemies to behold in His person the promised Messias, by asking them what they thought of Him Whom they all expected, and whose son they believed He was to be.

Q. Did the Pharisees give a correct answer when they said that the Christ was to be the son of David?

A. They answered correctly in part, but not in full. The Messias was true God and true man, and hence they should have said: As God, the Christ was the son of the Eternal Father; and as man, He was a descendant of the house of David. But the Pharisees either did not know or did not want to believe in the divinity of Jesus Christ; therefore they gave only a partial answer. The Divine Master, however, did not omit to place this great truth before them, and convinced them in such a manner that no one was able to answer Him a word.

Q. With what argument did He silence them?

A. By showing them that David, inspired by the Holy Ghost, called the Christ his Lord, thus giving Him a title which he would not have given Him if he had not known Him to be greater than he himself, because He was the Son of God, Who was to make His enemies His footstool. In this way He proved His divinity and showed them the triumph which He was to have over them.

Q. What are we to learn from this Gospel?

A. We are to learn that our first and greatest duty is to love God above all things and our neighbor as ourselves. We are to learn further not to question or cavil with God on the maxims of religion. Lastly, we are to learn how great our confusion will be, if, like the Pharisees, we dare to impugn anything that redounds to the glory of Jesus Christ.

EIGHTEENTH SUNDAY AFTER PENTECOST.

Gospel: St. Matthew ix. 1–8.

AT that time: "Jesus, entering into a boat, passed over the water and came into His own city. And behold they brought to Him one sick of the palsy lying in a bed. And Jesus, seeing their faith, said to the man sick of the palsy: Be of good heart, son, thy sins are forgiven thee. And behold some of the scribes said within themselves: He blasphemeth. And Jesus, seeing their thoughts, said: Why do you think evil in your hearts? Whether is easier, to say, Thy sins are forgiven thee: or to say, Arise and walk? But that you may know that the Son of man hath power on earth to forgive sins, (then saith He to the man sick of the palsy:) Arise, take up thy bed, and go into thy house. And he arose, and went into his house. And the multitude seeing it, feared, and glorified God that gave such power to men."

Q. What city was that which Jesus went to?

A. It was the city of Capharnaum, on the west bank of the river Jordan, a little before it flows into the Sea of Tiberias, also called the Lake of Genesareth and the Sea of Galilee. This was a rich commercial city, and the emporium of all Judea on account of its great population, its extensive trade, and the concourse of strangers.

Q. Why does the Evangelist call Capharnaum the city of Jesus, saying: "He came into His own city"?

A. The home of Jesus was Nazareth, but St. John Chrysostom and many others are of the opinion that He cherished a special affection for Capharnaum, so that St. Matthew called it His city. In Capharnaum there was a house where Christ was accustomed to meet with His apostles, and in this city He began to preach the kingdom of God, to correct the prevailing vices, to teach virtue, and worked many astounding miracles.

Q. What miracles did Christ perform in Capharnaum?

A. He healed the paralytic mentioned in the Gospel, He restored sight to two blind persons, and healed the deaf and dumb man who was possessed by the devil, of which mention is made in the Gospel for the third Sunday in Lent. He also cured the servant of the centurion, the woman who was suffering from a loss of blood, and the son of Regulus, who was dying of fever. Besides these, He recalled to life the daughter of Jairus.

Q. Of whom was this paralytic a figure?

A. He was a figure of the human race, which was sick on account of the sin of its first parent. This paralytic was in a pitiable condition; he could not take a step, or even stand. He could not use his hands, and he was incurable by natural means. In like manner the human race was reduced to a most deplorable condition; it could not withstand the power of the passions, it could not take a step or do anything by which to gain heaven, and no one could help it but Jesus Christ alone.

Q. Why did Jesus say to the man: "Be of good heart, thy sins are forgiven thee"?

A. The health of his body would have been of little account to him if he had not received with it the health of his soul; therefore Jesus first gave him the most necessary grace, that is, the health of his soul, and then that of less importance, the health of his body.

Q. What are we to learn from this?

A. We are to learn that when we are sick our first thought should be to place ourselves in the grace of God, thus healing our soul first, because diseases are very often a punishment for sins committed; hence a cure can scarcely be hoped for if the cause has not first been removed by repentance.

Q. What are we to think of those who said that Jesus blasphemed when He said, "Thy sins are forgiven thee"?

A. We need not be surprised at this. Ignorant people call all things they do not understand blunders and folly; so also do unbelievers and the wicked call blasphemy every truth of faith which they do not comprehend or which they do not like. Those scribes did not know, or did not want to know, that Jesus was God, and when He said that the sins of the paralytic were forgiven him, these words seemed to them to be a horrible blasphemy. How many Christians also accuse the ministers of the altar of rigorism, scrupulosity, and ignorance, when they announce truths that are not according to the taste of their corrupt hearts, or which appear new to them, because they never learned their religion as they should.

Q. Why did Jesus rebuke their secret thoughts?

A. This appears to be a rebuke, but in reality it was for them a great charity, because, as God alone can penetrate the secrets of the heart and mind, Jesus, by showing that He knew their secret thoughts, gave them a convincing proof that He was truly God. Sinners also may learn from this that no matter how much they strive to hide themselves before men, God always knows them, for He searches the innermost recesses of the heart.

Q. What else did Christ show in this case?

A. By the fact itself He showed that, on account of His divinity and the merits of His passion, He had the power of forgiving sins and of assisting sinners by His grace to obtain the victory over their passions and to walk on the road to heaven, like the paralytic who arose healthy and sound, took up his bed, and went into his house.

Q. Of what, therefore, was the paralytic a figure on this occasion?

A. He was a figure of mankind restored to grace by Jesus Christ, risen again from the weakness to which it had been reduced by the sin of its first parent, fortified against its passions, and rendered able to walk on the way of salvation toward its home, paradise.

Q. Of what was he more particularly an image?

A. St. Gregory says: The bed upon which the paralytic lay prostrate and unable to move signified the carnal passions in which the soul of a sinner lies abandoned and unable to do any good. The paralytic, in carrying his bed and going into his house, is a figure of the sinner who, being converted and placed in the state of grace, rises from the mire of his passions, carries triumphantly the weight of temptations, strives in works of penance, walks in the path of justice, and returns to that house which is prepared for him in heaven by the merits of Jesus Christ.

Q. What are we to learn from this Gospel?

A. The miserable condition of the paralytic teaches us to fear the misery to which our sinful passions can reduce us. The kindness with which the Divine Redeemer treated the sick man invites us to have great confidence in God, and to trust in His mercy even if we are great sinners. The greatness of the miracle causes us to admire the great power conferred by Jesus Christ on the priests in order that they may use it in a spiritual manner in the sacrament of penance; and the whole history teaches us to fear, to give thanks, and to glorify God, and Him Whom He sent to dwell among us, Jesus Christ, His only Son, Our Lord.

NINETEENTH SUNDAY AFTER PENTECOST.

Gospel: St. Matthew xxii. 2-14.

AT that time: Jesus spoke to the chief priests and Pharisees in parables, saying: "The kingdom of heaven is likened to a king, who made a marriage for his son. And he sent his servants to call them that were invited to the marriage: and they would not come. Again he sent other servants, saying: Tell them that were invited: Behold, I have prepared my dinner; my beeves and fatlings are killed, and all things are ready: come ye to the marriage. But they neglected, and went their ways, one to his farm and another to his merchandise. And the rest laid hands on his servants, and, having treated them contumeliously, put them to death. But when the king had heard of it he was angry, and, sending his armies, he destroyed those murderers, and burnt their city. Then he saith to his servants: The marriage indeed is ready: but they that were invited were not worthy. Go ye therefore into the highways; and as many as you shall find call to the marriage. And his servants, going forth into the highways, gathered together all that they found, both bad and good: and the marriage was filled with guests. And the king went in to see the guests: and he saw there a man who had not on a wedding garment. And he saith to him: Friend, how camest thou in hither not having a wedding garment? But he was silent. Then the king said to the waiters: Bind his hands and feet, and cast him into the exterior darkness: there shall be weeping and gnashing of teeth. For many are called, but few are chosen."

Q. What was the object of this parable?

A. It was to warn the Jews of the danger and of the fatal consequences of their obstinacy in refusing to recognize in Him that Messias Who came to call them in the name of His Eternal Father to partake of the kingdom of heaven.

Q. What does the kingdom of heaven signify, who is the king, and who is the bridegroom?

A. The kingdom of heaven is the Church, in which God exercises His power over the minds and hearts; the royal father who prepares the nuptial feast is the same God Who invites all mankind to enter the Church, and the bridegroom is Jesus Christ, true God and true man, Who is united to the Church by the strongest ties.

Q. What are we to understand by the nuptial feast?

A. That most bountiful feast of eternal life which is received in the Church, whether of doctrine, of grace, or of the merits of Jesus Christ.

Q. Why is such a feast said to be prepared by the royal father?

A. Because the holy Church was ordained and prepared by God from all eternity, and God sent His only begotten Son to become man to complete the great work begun by Him.

Q. Who are the invited, and who are they who did not accept the first invitation?

A. The invited are all the children of Adam, as well of the Old as of the New Dispensation, and those who refused the first invitation were principally the Gentiles, who did not believe in the Christ Who was to come, and did not profit by the example of the chosen people. They were also the Jews, who did not listen to the voice of the prophets, and refused to acknowledge the promised and expected Messias. Lastly, they are all those who did not and do not accept the truths of the gospel.

Q. Who were the servants sent out by the king to give the first invitation?

A. They were the prophets who invited men to believe and to hope in the Messias, and who announced His coming, His sanctity, His miracles, and all the circumstances of His birth, life, passion, and death.

Q. Who were those sent to renew the invitation?

A. They were the apostles and all their legitimate successors in the preaching of the gospel, and they are now all the ministers of the altar who announce the divine word and invite the people to drink with joy from the rich fountains of the Saviour.

Q. What do the animals that were killed for the feast signify?

A. All this food, which indicates the wealth and sumptuousness of an earthly table, signifies the abundance and the excellence of the food which God has prepared for our souls in the Church.

Q. How do we prove this abundance?

A. If we consider the promises of God made to the patriarchs, the predictions of the prophets, the figures of the sacrifices and of the legal ceremonies, and the foreshadowings in the events and in the famous personages of the Hebrew nation, we shall see with what abundance God prepared the nuptial feast of Jesus Christ; that is, how many lights and how many means He prepared, in order that the promised Saviour might be known when in the fulness of time He should appear among men.

Q. Does this abundance stop here?

A. Certainly not. If we consider the doctrines of Jesus Christ, His miracles, His example, His death, His merits, and His sacraments, the preaching of the apostles, the constancy of the martyrs, the prodigies which signalized the promulgation of the faith and the constant assistance of the Holy Ghost, we shall comprehend how abundantly God has provided food for our souls, for our faith, our hope, our charity, our perfection; in a word, for the nuptials of the Church with the heavenly Spouse.

Q. Who are they who maltreated the servants?

A. First, they are the Jews, who stoned the prophets and crucified Christ. Secondly, they are the persecutors of the Church, who condemned the promulgators of the gospel to all kinds of torments; and lastly, they are those who persecute the priests because they are the ministers of God and the teachers of religion.

Q. How was the revenge of the angry king realized in regard to the Jews?

A. You find the answer in the ruins of the city of Jerusalem, and in the Jews themselves, scattered over the face of the earth without throne or temple.

Q. Who are they who were called from all parts and partook of the marriage-feast?

A. They were the Gentiles and the people of every nation who, called by the apostles to the profession of the gospel, embraced the holy faith and filled the Church of Jesus Christ.

Q. Of whom was the man a figure who had not on a nuptial garment?

A. He was the sad image of all those who are indeed in the Church because they have been baptized, but who have not the nuptial garment; that is, who have not justice and sanctifying grace, because they are in the state of mortal sin.

Q. Why did the king call that man a friend?

A. From this we may learn that God hates sin, but not the sinner; because, although he is His enemy by sin, still he is His creature, created unto His likeness, and redeemed by the blood of Jesus Christ; therefore He is inclined to treat him in a friendly manner whenever, accepting the invitation of His grace, he will ask pardon for his sins and provide himself by repentance with the nuptial garment, which he has not when in the state of sin.

Q. Why, then, did he sentence him to be punished?

A. In order to warn us that the sinner who is mute and does not confess his guilt and ask for pardon, as this man in the Gospel, will be banished from eternal joy, and will be sentenced to be cast out of the kingdom into eternal pain.

Q. What are we to learn from this parable of the Gospel?

A. We are to learn principally three things: first, not to despise divine grace: second, to be sure that we have the nuptial garment, which is sanctifying grace; and lastly, that it is not enough to be in the Church and to bear the name of Christian in order to be saved, as it was not sufficient for that man to be seated at the nuptial banquet, from which he was ignominiously banished.

TWENTIETH SUNDAY AFTER PENTECOST.

Gospel: St. John iv. 46–53.

AT that time: "There was a certain ruler whose son was sick at Capharnaum. He having heard that Jesus was come from Judea into Galilee, went to Him, and prayed Him to come down and heal his son, for he was at the point of death. Jesus therefore said to him: Unless you see signs and wonders you believe not. The ruler saith to him: Lord, come down before that my son die. Jesus saith to him: Go thy way, thy son liveth. The man believed the word which Jesus said to him, and went his way. And as he was going down his servants met him; and they brought word, saying that his son lived. He asked therefore of them the hour wherein he grew better. And they said to him: Yesterday at the seventh hour the fever left him. The father therefore knew that it was at the same hour that Jesus said to him, Thy son liveth; and himself believed, and his whole house."

Q. Where did Jesus work this miracle, and where was this ruler from?

A. Jesus worked this miracle in the city of Cana in Galilee, where He had converted water into wine. The ruler was from Capharnaum, which is situated at the north-western side of the Lake of Genesareth, many miles distant from Cana. Capharnaum was a city loved by the Divine Teacher, and one which He had made famous by many miracles.

Q. Why did Christ rebuke that man, saying: "Unless you see signs and wonders you believe not"?

A. He did this to show the ruler the imperfection of his faith, for if he really believed that Christ was true God he would have known that a simple act of His all-powerful will was sufficient to cure his dying son, and that it was not necessary for the sick son to be present in person. This reproof was given, however, not only to him, but also to all who thought like him, and whose faith was as imperfect as his was.

Q. Did this rebuke open the eyes of the ruler to see the imperfection of his faith?

A. No; but he renewed his prayer and requested the Divine Teacher to come down to his house before his son died. How many Christians, even in our day, by applying to others the reproofs which they should apply to themselves, continue in their defects without correcting themselves as they should.

Q. Was Christ vexed because the ruler persisted in his imperfect faith?

A. He was not vexed, but in His mercy He chose rather to cure his mind by hearing his prayer and by working the miracle without moving from the place where He was. Let us admire here the patience and the goodness of Our Lord Jesus Christ, Who had compassion for human infirmities, and bestowed His favors even on those who were imperfect.

Q. Why did He refuse to go to Capharnaum? Was the journey difficult?

A. He did not mind the inconvenience of such a journey, but He knew very well that if He then and at such a distance cured the sick son, He would thereby prove that He was God, Who sees and controls absent things as if they were present, it being sufficient for Him to say: "Go, thy son liveth."

Q. Was the ruler's faith perfected by these words of Christ?

A. The ruler believed the words of the Divine Teacher, and, therefore, his faith increased; still, as we can gather from the Gospel, his faith was as yet not perfect.

Q. When did his faith become perfect?

A. When the ruler heard from his servants, who had come in haste to meet their master, that the fever had suddenly left his dying son the day before at the seventh hour, that is, one hour after midday, and, therefore, at the very same moment when Christ had assured him that his son would live, then he was convinced that Christ was truly the Son of God; that He was almighty, and the Lord of life and death; he believed Him to be the expected Messias, and he and his whole family sincerely embraced the faith of the gospel.

Q. Of whom were the ruler, his sick son, and the fever figures?

A. Some sacred interpreters recognize, in this ruler who left his home to seek Christ, the human mind as a queen in the midst of all things created, which naturally rises above all material things, and, leaving far behind what is subject to the senses, goes in search of the truth that comes from heaven. In the ruler's sick son they recognize the human will, weak and wavering in the midst of the seduction of the world; and in the fever they recognize the power of the passions, which corrupt the will and cause it to be almost without life in regard to doing good.

Q. What are we to learn from this Gospel?

A. First, we are to learn how useful trials and afflictions are to lead us to God, for the ruler and his whole house would perhaps not have believed in Jesus Christ if the son had not been afflicted with that mortal sickness. Secondly, we are to admire the goodness of God in bearing with our imperfections when we pray to Him; and lastly, like that ruler, we are to lead our neighbor, at least by our good example, to the knowledge of God and to the faithful observance of His holy law.

TWENTY-FIRST SUNDAY AFTER PENTECOST.

Gospel: St. Matthew xviii. 23-35.

AT that time, Jesus spoke to His disciples this parable: "The kingdom of heaven is likened to a king, who would take an account of his servants. And when he had begun to take the account, one was brought to him that owed him ten thousand talents. And as he had not wherewith to pay it, his lord commanded that he should be sold, and his wife and children, and all that he had, and payment to be made. But that servant, falling down, besought him, saying: Have patience with me, and I will pay thee all. And the lord of that servant, being moved with pity, let him go and forgave him the debt. But when that servant was gone out, he found one of his fellow-servants that owed him a hundred pence; and laying hold of him, he throttled him, saying: Pay what thou owest. And his fellow-servant, falling down, besought him, saying: Have patience with me, and I will pay thee all. And he would not, but went and cast him into prison, till he paid the debt. Now his fellow-servants, seeing what was done, were very much grieved, and they came and told their lord all that was done. Then his lord called him, and said to him: Thou wicked servant! I forgave thee all the debt, because thou besoughtest me: shouldst not thou then have had compassion also on thy fellow-servant, even as I had compassion on thee? And his lord being angry, delivered him to the torturers until he paid all the debt. So also shall My Heavenly Father do to you, if you forgive not every one his brother from your hearts."

Q. Of whom are this king and the debtor in the parable figures?

A. As in all the other parables so in this the king is a figure of God, master and judge of the universe; and the debtor represents sinful man, who must render an account of all his actions to the Divine Justice.

Q. Why is this servant represented as being so heavily in debt?

A. It is evident that the Divine Master thus represented him in order to express the enormity of sin, and the immense debt contracted with God by him who commits it.

Q. What fault had the wife and children committed, that they also were to be sold?

A. This is an ornament of the parable, founded on the practice of certain very singular cases, as can be seen in Daniel. At any rate it may well signify that sometimes a whole family and an entire community must suffer for the sin of a father or of a member, in the same manner as all who were in the ship with the prophet Jonas were in danger of drowning, because he had been disobedient to God. All Egypt was punished on account of Pharao, and three thousand conquerors of Jericho were put to flight near the city Hai by a handful of uncircumcised men, on account of one only, Achan.

Q. How could the poor servant promise to pay so large a sum?

A. Strictly speaking, it was impossible for him to pay such an enormous debt, but this was said to signify that a sinner, although he cannot do anything of himself, can truly promise to satisfy the Divine Justice, relying on the infinite treasure of the passion and merits of Jesus Christ.

Q. How could the king be so easily moved to compassion and forgive so great a debt?

A. From this we should learn how great is the goodness of God, and how willingly He forgives him who sincerely confesses his sins and firmly resolves to amend his life. David and Magdalen are very eloquent examples of this.

Q. Of whom is that servant a figure who refused to have pity on his fellow-servant?

A. In this particular he is a figure of those Christians who refuse to forgive their neighbor, whilst they themselves dare to hope, or have even previously obtained the forgiveness of their sins, which are far more grievous.

Q. What are we to think of him when we see him having recourse to the tribunals to obtain satisfaction?

A. By acting in this manner he is the odious picture of those vindictive persons who make use of all imaginable means to obtain satisfaction for injuries received, and it makes us feel how disgraceful and revolting such conduct is.

Q. Why did his fellow-servants inform their master of the bad conduct of this man?

A. This signifies that the true servants of the Lord are always displeased and sorry for the acts of revenge done by Christians, and that, however just the satisfaction obtained may appear to be, the heavenly Master will always know it, will judge it rigorously, and will discover the secret malice thereof.

Q. But this master did not oblige the servant to cancel the obligations due him from others. Why, then, was he so angry with him?

A. Let us learn from this how angry the Lord will be with us if we exact satisfaction, knowing that He has strictly commanded us to forgive our neighbor from our heart, and that He has repeatedly assured us that we shall be treated by Him in the same manner as we have treated others.

Q. Why did the master deliver that servant to the torturers?

A. The Divine Teacher said this in the parable to let us know that whosoever does not sincerely forgive his enemies will be sentenced to the torments of hell.

Q. What are we to learn from this Gospel?

A. In the first place, we are to learn to acknowledge before God our great debts, that is, our sins, with sincerity and humility of heart. Secondly, we are to learn to have a firm purpose of making good our great debt as far as we can with the assistance of divine grace, by repentance, by receiving the holy sacraments, and by other good works. Lastly, we are to learn sincerely to pardon those who have offended us, and to fear the punishments with which God has threatened vindictive men.

TWENTY-SECOND SUNDAY AFTER PENTECOST.

Gospel: St. Matthew xxii. 15–21.

AT that time: "The Pharisees going, consulted among themselves how to ensnare Jesus in His speech. And they sent to Him their disciples with the Herodians, saying: Master, we know that Thou art a true speaker, and teachest the way of God in truth, neither carest Thou for any man: for Thou dost not regard the person of men. Tell us therefore what dost Thou think, Is it lawful to give tribute to Cæsar or not? But Jesus, knowing their wickedness, said: Why do you tempt Me, ye hypocrites? Show me the coin of the tribute. And they offered Him a penny. And Jesus saith to them: Whose image and inscription is this? They say to Him, Cæsar's. Then He saith to them: Render therefore to Cæsar the things that are Cæsar's, and to God the things that are God's."

Q. For what purpose did the Pharisees and Herodians present themselves before our Divine Teacher?

A. They approached Him with the perfidious design of catching Him in His words, and of finding in His reply to their question an excuse to condemn Him and make Him odious to one or the other of the opposing parties.

Q. What was their question, and what did the Jews think of the point involved?

A. The question was this: Is it lawful for the Jews to pay tribute to Cæsar? To this the Hebrews were very much opposed, because a great part of them submitted unwillingly to the law imposing the tribute; and still more, following the teachings of a certain Gaulonite, were of the opinion that it was not lawful for the Hebrew nation to pay tribute to the Gentiles, and that to do so was for them a sin.

Q. To what danger was Jesus Christ exposed in answering the question?

A. If He declared it to be lawful to pay tribute to the Romans He would have made Himself odious to the Jews, and most odious to the followers of the Gaulonite, the leader of those zealots who afterward caused so much misery to unfortunate Jerusalem. And if, on the contrary, He declared it unlawful to pay the tribute, He would have provoked the anger and invited the vengeance of Cæsar, and the enmity and persecution of Herod, a great partisan of the emperor.

Q. What are we to think of the great praise the Jews and Herodians bestowed on our Divine Master?

A. The praise was due to Jesus Christ, Who merited it in the strictest and highest sense of the term; but on the part of those perfidious hypocrites it was a stroke of the most refined malice and an insidious trap to cause Him to fall. They hoped, by blinding Him with flattery, to lead Him rashly to give a decision that would offend one or the other party.

Q. But Jesus Christ reproved and confounded them?

A. The reproof which our Divine Master gave them arose not from anger or a spirit of revenge; it was rather an act of charity, because in doing this He showed Himself a scrutinizer of the mind and heart, and gave them an occasion of enlightenment, repentance, and salvation, if they had reflected and profited by it. A superior should not withhold a reproof from him who does wrong when it may prove beneficial to the wrong-doer or to those who are present.

Q. What do you observe in this reply of Jesus Christ?

A. We see and admire a divine prudence, for by this answer, and without offending one party or the other, He taught the obedience due to those in authority, and enlightened the conscience of the Jews, by calming the opposition of the one and the scruples of the other.

Q. Did Jesus Christ on this occasion teach us something else?

A. Yes; He taught us to give sincerely to our superiors due obedience in all things, and to render to God as a tribute that soul which is marked with His image and with the indelible characters of the holy sacraments.

Q. What are we to learn from this Gospel?

A. We are taught in the first place not to try to deceive our neighbor by feigned praise and adulation, as in our day is done by many. We are also taught not to put our trust in the praises of men. We are, moreover, taught not to give our opinion too rashly; not to offend the opinion of others and enforce our own; and lastly, we are taught to show ourselves' obedient subjects of authority and sincere worshippers of our God.

TWENTY-THIRD SUNDAY AFTER PENTECOST.

Gospel: St. Matthew ix. 18-26.

AT that time: "As Jesus was speaking these things unto them, behold a certain ruler came up, and adored Him, saying: Lord, my daughter is even now dead; but come, lay Thy hand upon her, and she shall live. And Jesus rising up followed him with His disciples. And behold a woman who was troubled with an issue of blood twelve years came behind Him, and touched the hem of His garment. For she said within herself: If I shall touch only His garment, I shall be healed. But Jesus turning and seeing her, said: Be of good heart, daughter, thy faith hath made thee whole.

And the woman was made whole from that hour. And when Jesus was come into the house of the ruler, and saw the minstrels and the multitude making a rout He said: Give place, for the girl is not dead, but sleepeth. And they laughed Him to scorn. And when the multitude was put forth, He went in and took her by the hand. And the maid arose. And the fame hereof went abroad into all that country."

Q. First of all, was this girl dead?

A. In reading the account of this same event in the other Gospels it appears that when this man, whom Luke calls Jairus, left home, his daughter was dying, and that as he was returning with Jesus Christ to Capharnaum he met the servants who brought him the sad news of her death. So that when our divine Lord arrived at the house of Jairus the daughter had ceased to live.

Q. In how many different senses may this Gospel be understood?

A. In three: literal, allegorical, and moral. It is first to be understood in a literal sense, because the facts related are literally true. In the second place, it can be interpreted in an allegorical sense, because these facts are symbolic of still greater things in the order of grace; and lastly, these same facts, taken in a moral sense, indicate things which we should do.

Q. Whom does Jairus symbolize?

A. Jairus, who conducted Jesus to the house where his daughter lay dead, was a leader in the provincial synagogue at Capharnaum. He was a figure of Moses, who was the leader and ruler of the Hebrew people, and who by his government and legislation prepared the way for the advent of the Messias, Who was to come into the world and into the house of Jacob, and Who was to give life to the human race, dead through the sin of Adam, but, unlike the fallen angels, capable of resurrection through the grace of the Redeemer.

Q. And whom does the infirm woman represent?

A. Remember that this woman, who for twelve years could not be cured by all the efforts of the medical art, was unclean according to the law, and was cured on the public street by touching the garment of our Divine Redeemer, and she obtained this grace before the girl who was dead. This infirm woman, then, was an image of the Gentile people, spiritually infirm for so long a time, without any of their philosophers being able to lead them to salvation; impure by their superstitions, and by their shameful customs placed outside of the house of Jacob and wandering in the way of perdition, but cured by their approach to Jesus Christ and by recognizing Him as true God and man, and led to the spiritual life before the Hebrews, always obstinate in the shadow of death.

Q. And the girl, first sick and then dead, whom does she represent?

A. This girl symbolizes the synagogue, or the Hebrew people, in this way: The Hebrews had in their midst the Messias, but, actuated by their prepossessions and blinded by their passions, they refused to recognize Him as such; they hated Him and persecuted Him to death. They were then dying before God and about to be rejected by Him. They had placed Him on the cross and set themselves against accepting Him as the promised Christ, and thus they were dead in the eyes of the God of their fathers.

Q. Why then did Christ say that the girl, the image of the synagogue, was not dead, but only sleeping?

A. The girl was really dead, but, because the Divine Redeemer had determined to resuscitate her, He compared her death to a sleep, and said she slept, indicating that she would awake and return to the duties of life.

Q. How can you apply this to the Hebrew people?

A. At present the Hebrews, obstinate in their blindness, are outside of the Church, are deprived of sanctifying grace, and sleep the sleep of death; but before the end of the world they will awake from their deep lethargy, adore Jesus crucified, enter into the Church, and will be of the one fold and one shepherd. Thus the Hebrew nation is not entirely dead forever; now it sleeps in its incredulity, but one day it will be aroused and called into life by the grace of the Redeemer. We say, then, in reference to it: The child is not dead, but sleepeth.

Q. In a moral sense, what do we see in the woman infirm for twelve years?

A. We see in this woman the sad image of a soul grown old in sin, a soul to which the services of the priest, good or terrible examples, and experience, whether prosperous or unfortunate, have been for a long time of no benefit.

Q. What is to be said about the sudden cure by touching the garment of Christ?

A. As the mystic garment of the Incarnate Word is His most holy humanity, we can see how great is the efficacy of the Most Holy Sacrament to cure a sinner of his spiritual maladies; also all those grown old in sin if they put themselves in the way of penance and seek in this sacrament the proper remedy.

Q. Why did Jesus Christ, as St. Mark tells us, oblige the infirm woman to make known her infirmity?

A. He did this in order that sinners should learn to confess with sincerity and courage to the priests, the dispensers of His graces, their spiritual infirmities, howsoever enormous and shameful, in order to obtain mercy, pardon, and perfect cure.

Q. And the dead girl, what did she represent?

A. She represented a soul recently fallen into mortal sin through frailty, surprise, or the violence of temptation, rather than through malice or depravity of heart.

Q. And did Christ on this account say that she was not dead, but asleep?

A. Yes; because God ordinarily by His mercy calls souls suddenly, principally by a great remorse, to a sincere repentance and a prompt return to the state of grace; and the time of their spiritual death being of short duration, they may be said to be asleep rather than dead.

Q. Were there many present at the resurrection of this girl?

A. According to St. Mark, there were present her relations and the three apostles, Peter, James, and John, the crowd having been sent out.

Q. How many did Jesus Christ raise from the dead?

A. Not all the miracles of Jesus Christ are recorded in the Gospels, and therefore we find only three raised from the dead, namely, the girl of twelve years, the son of the widow of Naim, and Lazarus of Bethania, the brother of Martha and Mary.

Q. Had these three dead persons the same signification?

A. No. The girl, as has been said, represented a soul fallen into grievous sin through frailty rather than through malice; the son of the widow signified an habitual sinner borne to perdition by his vices, to resuscitate whom a very great grace is necessary; and Lazarus represented a sinner grown old in iniquity and corrupted by the passions, for whose conversion it requires almost a miracle of grace.

Q. What are we to learn from the whole of this Gospel?

A. We learn to have recourse to Jesus Christ in all our needs with a lively faith and with humility, as had the ruler and the infirm woman. We should also admire the great goodness of our Divine Redeemer, Who was so prompt to console those who asked Him; He will do the same for us if we ask Him from our hearts. Lastly, as our Divine Master sent away the musicians from the bed of the dead girl, so we on the occasion of death should seek help for the soul, and not the noise and clamor and the vain pomp of the world.

TWENTY-FOURTH AND LAST SUNDAY AFTER PENTECOST.

Gospel: St. Matthew xxiv. 15-35.

AT that time, Jesus said to His disciples: "When therefore you shall see the abomination of desolation, which was spoken of by Daniel the prophet, standing in the holy place, he that readeth, let him understand. Then they that are in Judea, let them flee to the mountains. And he that is on the house-top, let him not come down to take anything out of his house. And he that is in the field, let him not go back to take his coat. And woe to them that are with child, and that give suck in those days. But pray that your flight be not in the winter, or on the Sabbath. For there shall be then great tribulation, such as hath not been from the beginning of the world until now, neither shall be. And unless those days had been shortened, no flesh should be saved: but for the sake of the elect those days shall be shortened. Then if any man shall say to you: Lo here is Christ, or there, do not believe him. For there shall arise false Christs and false prophets, and shall show great signs and wonders, in so much as to deceive (if possible) even the elect. Behold I have told it to you beforehand. If therefore they shall say to you: Behold He is in the desert, go ye not out; behold He is in the closets, believe it not. For as lightning cometh out of the East, and appeareth even unto the West, so shall also the coming of the Son of man be. Wheresoever the body shall be, there shall the eagles also be gathered together. And immediately after the tribulation of those days the sun shall be darkened, and the moon shall not give her light, and the stars shall fall from heaven, and the powers of heaven shall be moved. And then shall appear the sign of the Son of man in heaven: and then shall all the tribes of the earth mourn: and they shall see the Son of man coming in the clouds of heaven with much power and majesty. And He shall send His angels with a trumpet, and a great voice: and they shall gather together His elect from the four winds, from the farthest parts of the heavens to the utmost bounds of them. And from the fig-tree learn a parable: when the branch thereof is now tender, and the leaves come forth, you know that summer is nigh. So you also, when you shall see all these things, know ye that it is nigh, even at the doors. Amen, I say to you, that this generation shall not pass till all these things be done. Heaven and earth shall pass away, but My words shall not pass."

Q. What is the object of this discourse of Christ?

A. Christ had two things in view. One was to advise His followers among the Jews to escape the evils that were to come over Jerusalem, and the other was to warn Christians who will be living at the end of the world to be prepared for the great desolation that will precede His second coming, when He will come to judge the living and the dead. For this reason does the Divine Master foretell the calamities that will befall the obstinate city of Jerusalem before her entire destruction; and He predicts the dreadful events that will take place when the end of the world and the dreadful day of judgment are near at hand.

Q. In regard to the Jews, what is the abomination mentioned in this Gospel?

A. This abomination foretold by Daniel (chap. ix.) in regard to the Jews has reference to the strife, the murders, sacrileges, and all kinds of crimes committed by the different factions, more especially by that of the so-called "Zealots," not only in the streets and squares of the holy city, but also in the very temple. The crimes committed by them in the days preceding the fall of Jerusalem are so horrible that they may truly be called the abominations of desolation; that is, abominations that are the forerunners of the approaching desolation.

Q. In regard to Christians, of what abomination did Christ speak?

A. He spoke of that abomination which will be caused by all sorts of crimes, and which, like a mighty torrent, will overflow the earth in the days of Antichrist, who will appear at the end of the world.

Q. What counsel did Christ give the Jews who believed in Him?

A. He most earnestly advised them to flee as soon as possible in order not to be overtaken by the calamities that were to befall Jerusalem, as, in fact, the Christians did who were in the city and environs at the first sight of the Roman army.

Q. What did Christ, by the same words, mean to say to the Christians who will live at the end of the world?

A. He counsels them to flee from the general corruption that will reign supreme with Anti-christ, even at the cost of what is most dear to them on this earth, preferring to lose all temporal things rather than lose their souls and forfeit the imperishable goods of heaven.

Q. What do these words mean: "Woe to them that are with child, and that give suck in those days.

But pray that your flight be not in winter or on the Sabbath"?

A. In reference to the Jews these words signify the extreme danger they would incur during the siege of the city, and as mothers and nurses are unable to travel far, and as it would be impossible to undertake a long journey in winter or on the Sabbath, which last was forbidden by the law, He spoke to them in this manner to make them understand how necessary it was to leave hastily that city devoted to destruction.

Q. What do those words mean in regard to us?

A. He whose heart is controlled by passions which cause him to commit all kinds of sin, who cherishes carnal affections, and is attached to the things of this world, cannot walk as he ought in the way of salvation. On this account Christ said: Woe to those who will not be able to escape the torrent of iniquity that will overflow the earth, especially in the days of Anti-christ. In telling them to pray that their flight may not be in winter or on the Sabbath He advised the sinners not to delay their conversion and necessary penance to old age, symbolized by winter; and much less should they defer them until their last sickness or last day of life, symbolized by the Sabbath, for in such a case they would risk dying impenitent for want of time or of strength, and thus be the victims of eternal desolation.

Q. Who are the false prophets mentioned by Christ?

A. In regard to the Jews they were those who, during and after the affliction of Jerusalem, endeavored to deceive the people by pretending they were the expected Messias, foremost among whom was one

Barcocheba. In regard to us the false prophets are the teachers of false doctrines, of heresies, and of bad morals, who always have endeavored to change the truths of the gospel, and who will exert their whole strength and power to that effect in the days of Anti-christ, at the end of the world.

Q. What are we to learn from all this?

A. Considering how all the predictions in regard to Jerusalem were most minutely fulfilled, we understand why Jesus Christ said that heaven and earth shall pass away, but that His words shall not pass away. Moreover, let us learn to fear the dreadful punishments of the anger of God, to do penance for our sins, to avoid the occasions of sin, and to prepare ourselves for the day of judgment, of which the Gospel speaks, and which was explained on the first Sunday of Advent.

www.ingramcontent.com/pod-product-compliance
Lightning Source LLC
Chambersburg PA
CBHW022006220426
43663CB00007B/987